DIET
FOR A
CHANGING
CLIMATE

FOOD FOR THOUGHT

CHRISTY MIHALY AND SUE HEAVENRICH

TWENTY-FIRST CENTURY BOOKS / MINNEAPOLIS

This book is dedicated to all the young people who hold the future of the world in their hands. We hope that our words will help inspire new weed-eaters, invasivores, and entomophagists.

. . . and especially to Abigail, Nathan, Marina, and David —CM

. . . and to Lou for continued support and encouragement. (He does not know about the ants in the frittata yet.) —SH

A huge thank you to our fabulous editor at Twenty-First Century Books, Domenica Di Piazza, who nurtured this book so well from its buggy beginnings.

Twenty-First Century Books
A division of Lerner Publishing Group, Inc.
241 First Avenue North
Minneapolis, MN 55401 USA

For reading levels and more information, look up this title at www.lernerbooks.com.

Main body text set in Adrianna Condensed Regular 11/15.
Typeface provided by Chank.

Library of Congress Cataloging-in-Publication Data

Names: Mihaly, Christy, author. | Heavenrich, Sue, author.
Title: Diet for a changing climate : food for thought / Christy Mihaly, Sue Heavenrich.
Description: Minneapolis : Twenty-First Century Books, [2019] | Includes bibliographical references
    and index. | Audience: Age 13–18. | Audience: Grade 9 to 12. |
Identifiers: LCCN 2017043702 (print) | LCCN 2017046753 (ebook) | ISBN 9781541524774 (eb pdf) |
    ISBN 9781512481211 (library bound : alk. paper)
Subjects: LCSH: Food habits—Environmental aspects—Juvenile literature. | Diet—Juvenile literature. |
    Pests—Juvenile literature. | Local foods—Juvenile literature.
Classification: LCC GT2860 (ebook) | LCC GT2860 .M54 2019 (print) | DDC 613.2—dc23

LC record available at https://lccn.loc.gov/2017043702

Manufactured in the United States of America
1-43282-33106-4/2/2018

CONTENTS

INTRODUCTION

EARTH IS WARMING, SEAS ARE RISING, NATURAL HABITATS ARE VANISHING, AND DOZENS OF ENDANGERED PLANTS AND ANIMALS ARE DYING OUT EVERY DAY. Invasive organisms are destroying crops. Millions of people around the globe are losing their homes and crops because of flooding or drought. Millions more live in extreme poverty and are starving.

Sometimes the world's problems can seem overwhelming. The good news is that yes, you can make a difference. The challenges of climate change, habitat loss, poverty, and hunger are interrelated. They are all influenced by one thing that you can control: *what you eat*.

Following a diet for a changing climate requires rethinking what we consider food. We humans sit at the top of the global food chain. We are the planet's top predator species. That means that if enough of us change what we eat, together we can improve the health and well-being of the global community and our planet.

RETHINKING FOOD FOR THE TWENTY-FIRST CENTURY

Most people don't think of farms as a source of pollution. But in fact, 15 to 28 percent of emissions of greenhouse gases—the gases that trap heat in Earth's atmosphere—come from large-scale farms in the United States and other developed countries. That includes methane from cows and other livestock as they burp and expel gas from their bodies. It also includes carbon dioxide from the petroleum-fueled machinery that farmers use in their fields and for transporting goods to market.

By adapting the way we eat to include insects such as these fried crickets, we can impact the environment in a positive way. Raising insects consumes far fewer natural resources than other sources of protein such as cattle, pigs, and poultry.

Many modern agricultural practices contribute to environmental problems. For example, farmers clear huge swaths of forest lands to make way for new cropland and pastures. This deforestation leads to the loss of critical natural habitats for many animals. Cutting down trees, which absorb water and stabilize soil, worsens flooding and soil erosion. It also accelerates global warming. Leafy tree canopies that block the sun's rays keep the forest cool. And all those leaves absorb carbon dioxide, making forests critically important in the fight against climate change.

Industrial food production also requires large amounts of water. Often industrial farms raise only one type of crop. Without a variety of plants in the fields, crops are more vulnerable to pests. In addition, the soil is robbed of valuable nutrients. So farmers use huge amounts of pesticides and fertilizers to protect their crops from insects and to enrich the soil. When it rains, these toxins

Kudzu is an invasive vine that takes over a landscape quickly. The leaves are completely edible!

run into nearby waterways and pollute them, harming the plants and animals in the water. Meanwhile, droughts and harsh storms leave many small farmers struggling to raise enough food for their families and communities.

What can you do? Change your diet! Try embracing radical edibles to help save Earth. Experiment with mouthwatering meals you've never before encountered.

Pulling weeds and invasive kudzu vines from the garden and . . . eating them? Yes! Because these greens are local and nutritious, and treating them like trash is just tossing out good food.

Hunting iguanas for food? Yes! Because in southern states, invasive iguanas are devouring local vegetation and endangering the native species that rely on those plants . . . and it turns out iguana meat is good to eat.

Putting crickets and mealworms into recipes . . . on purpose? Yes! Raising insects requires less water and produces fewer climate-warming greenhouse gases than raising cattle and other livestock. And insects provide high-protein nutrition. In fact, the Food and Agriculture Organization of the United Nations says that one of the most effective ways to feed a hungry world is for more people to eat more insects.

FOOD FOR THOUGHT

Is eating kudzu and crickets radical? Right now it may be. But keep in mind that what at first seems subversive and gross often turns out to be cool later on. Really cool. It has happened before. Take lobster, for instance. Two hundred years ago, people thought lobsters were disgusting. In New England coastal states, people ground up lobsters to make fertilizer for their fields. They fed lobster meat to pigs and human prisoners. Today diners in restaurants pay high prices for lobster dinners.

If we want to find solutions in an age of climate change, it makes sense to learn more about where our food comes from and how it is grown. It makes sense to support less harmful ways of producing new foods that are tasty and nutritious. So, bring an open mind to the table. You might discover new tastes you love. More important, you'll be taking real action to solve global problems.

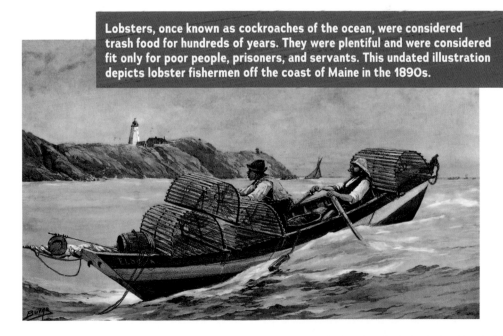

Lobsters, once known as cockroaches of the ocean, were considered trash food for hundreds of years. They were plentiful and were considered fit only for poor people, prisoners, and servants. This undated illustration depicts lobster fishermen off the coast of Maine in the 1890s.

CHAPTER 1

FOOD OUTSIDE YOUR FRONT DOOR

WHEN YOU THINK ABOUT COMBATING CLIMATE CHANGE, YOU PROBABLY THINK MOSTLY ABOUT SAVING ENERGY AND RELYING LESS ON CARS. These are great steps. But experts say that an even more effective way to reduce your carbon footprint—the amount of greenhouse gases you contribute to the atmosphere through your activities—is to focus on food. The locavore movement, for example, supports eating foods that are locally produced, often within 100 miles (160 km) of your home.

Eating local foods decreases emissions of greenhouse gases from the trucks that deliver crops to market. By driving shorter distances, they burn less fuel. So try shopping at a local farmers market. The food there comes from fields near or even in your community. And think wild! Maybe you've already plucked some juicy wild blackberries during a walk in the woods and popped them into your mouth. Closer to home, there's a good chance edible greens are growing right outside your door. Those dandelions sprouting in the yard and pushing their way through sidewalk cracks? They are packed with vitamins and minerals. Not only that, they taste good. Same with plantains, purslanes, mustards, and mallows—plants most people call weeds.

Outdoor markets, such as this one in southern France, are a perfect place to find fresh, local, and organic foods.

Weeds get a bad rap because they grow where we don't want them. They compete with other plants such as radishes or roses that we want to grow in our gardens. Or we want grass and nothing else on lawns, golf courses, and athletic fields. But that same dandelion or other "weed" growing elsewhere becomes a wildflower or a salad vegetable.

WHY EAT WEEDS?

Adventuresome chefs welcome the diversity of flavors that edible wild plants bring into their kitchens. Edible wild greens are packed with nutrients too. Leaf for leaf, many wild greens contain more nutrients than lettuce and other more familiar salad greens, beet greens, and spinach.

Eating weeds is good for the environment because these plants grow on their own, without human intervention. Weeds are volunteers that actually thrive in poor, even harsh, conditions. Nobody uses a tractor to prepare the soil for weeds or to plant weed seeds. Nobody intentionally waters or fertilizes them. In fact, every year homeowners in the United States spend close to $450 million on

NUTRIENTS IN 100 GRAMS (2 TO 3 CUPS) OF RAW GREENS*

The United States Department of Agriculture (USDA) measures nutrients in food by the gram. This chart compares nutritional values of 100 grams of some common greens.

	Calcium (mg)	Iron (mg)	Potassium (mg)	Vitamin C (mg)	Vitamin A IU
WILD PLANTS					
Chicory	100	0.9	420	24	5717
Dandelion	187	3.1	397	35	10161
Lamb's-quarter	309	1.2	452	80	11600
Mustards	115	1.34	384	70	3024
Purslane	65	1.99	494	21	1320
CULTIVATED CROPS					
Beet greens	117	2.57	762	30	6326
Leaf lettuce	36	0.86	194	9.2	7405
Spinach	99	2.71	558	28.1	9377

*Data from USDA National Nutrient Database for standard reference (ndb.nal.usda.gov/ndb/)

chemicals to kill weeds. That results in 28 million pounds (12.7 million kg) of active herbicide that gets washed off the lawn or percolates through the soil when it rains or when we water. Those chemicals eventually end up in our water supply.

We could save a lot of money—not to mention reduce chemical pollution—if, instead of spraying weeds, we ate them. When farmers see weeds as potential crops, they stop spraying weed killers. Sometimes they start harvesting the wild greens to sell alongside the cultivated crops they already send to market.

Best of all, because weeds grow in yards, playgrounds, and vacant lots, they are locally grown. Backyard weeds don't have to be trucked to market, processed, or packaged. Each of those steps requires energy and produces greenhouse gases. That means that when you toss local wild greens onto your salad or sandwich, you help cut down on greenhouse gas emissions and fight global warming.

STREET FOOD

When Philip Stark heads out for lunch in Berkeley, California, chances are he'll walk right by the food trucks without stopping. Instead, the street food he eats comes from sidewalk edges and vacant lots. Anywhere there's dirt, he says, you'll find something to eat. An amazing variety of edible plants grows in yards and weedy patches.

Stark is a professor of statistics at the University of California, Berkeley. He's also the principal investigator for the Berkeley Open Source Food (BOSF) project. He researches local edible weeds in Berkeley and neighboring West Oakland and Richmond. Stark is concerned about hunger—especially in low-income neighborhoods known as food deserts. These parts of town have few stores or markets selling fresh produce and other healthy foods.

The Berkeley Open Source Food project offers a colorful pamphlet to help foragers identify common wild greens.

The pineapple weed plant (*left*) has a distinctive cone-shaped flower head from which it gets its common name. The flower heads are tasty in salads and muffins and can be brewed as tea. The greens of the chickweed plant (*right*) are perfect for salads. When harvesting wild plants, be sure to avoid areas where pesticides and herbicides are used.

Fresh, free food grows all around us, Stark notes. He points to sow thistles (*Sonchus oleraceus*) with stems that can be cooked like asparagus and to pineapple weed (*Matricaria discoidea*) that smells as fragrant as its name suggests. "There's a myth that all weeds taste the same and are bitter," Stark says, "but they have a wide range of tastes." Mustard greens (Brassica family) taste peppery, chickweed (*Stellaria media*) tastes like alfalfa sprouts, and wood sorrel (*Oxalis* spp.) has a lemony tang ("spp." refers to multiple species).

Identifying edible plants is not difficult, Stark says. If you can distinguish leaf lettuce from Bibb lettuce in the produce aisle, you can learn to identify edible weeds. The problem for most people is that they don't recognize wild plants as food because they haven't ever seen them in a grocery store.

Stark and his BOSF colleagues work with farms, markets, and restaurants to create a supply chain bringing edible wild plants to consumers. Stark says some farms harvest weeds for local chefs. BOSF also publishes guides to the edible wild plants growing in urban neighborhoods around the Berkeley area. Their online field guide lists more than one hundred plants by their scientific and common names, with links to photos.

Many cultures take foraging (searching) for wild edible plants for granted. But in some neighborhoods in the United States, Stark says, people feel there is a stigma attached to foraging for wild edibles. To help inspire people to give eating weeds a try, BOSF leads plant walks through neighborhoods and parks. The project also hosts wild food celebrations. In addition, BOSF lobbies local government officials to try to persuade them to reduce the use of herbicides on public lands. The project also works with policy makers to change state, regional, and local laws to make it legal for people to pick—if not the daisies—at least the dandelions on public property. And to make sure that people don't eat contaminated plants, BOSF tests local urban soils for heavy metals and other pollutants and posts results on the project's website.

BOSF has also hosted tasting tables of wild edibles in food kitchens that serve homeless and low-income families. "One time we brought in bunches of chickweed to a food pantry," Stark reminisces. At first nobody wanted to take any—until a couple of people tried it and said that it tasted like salad. He shrugs. "It's hard for weeds to compete with junk food."

THERE'S AN APP FOR THAT

Electronic guides can help with wild food identification and recipes. One plant identification app, "Wild Edibles Forage," helps users identify and find recipes for more than 250 plants. The app includes detailed pictures of each plant, hundreds of photos, filters for season and habitat, and recipes. It also describes nonedible look-alikes to avoid. Crowdsourcing apps, such as "iNaturalist," allow users to share photos and locations of edible wild plants.

WHERE THE WILD THINGS GROW

Outside Seattle, Washington, Patti Pitcher harvests edible weeds and teaches foraging in her Farm Wife Mystery School. She cultivates vegetable gardens too. In early spring, the wild greens are ready to harvest long before her vegetable gardens begin producing. The greens she gathers from her yard are often the same plants that gardeners weed out of their rows of spinach and lettuces.

One of Pitcher's favorite weeds is gillie-across-the-ground. Other people call it gill-over-the-ground, creeping Charlie, alehoof, or ground ivy. "It's *Glechoma hederacea*," Pitcher says, calling the plant by its botanical name. "It stimulates digestion." This creeping plant is a perennial, so it comes back naturally year after year. It has a square stem, a clue that it is a member of the mint family. Early settlers brought it from Europe to North America for making tea and as a cough remedy. It is high in vitamin C, so Pitcher often adds its leaves to her soups.

Gillie leaves make great additions to salads. So do young and tender dandelion (*Taraxacum officinale*) and plantain leaves (*Plantago* spp.), chickweed, lamb's-quarter (*Chenopodium album*), and the flowers and leaves of various kinds of mustard greens. "Wild mustards are great for adding a zing of flavor," Pitcher says. One of her salad greens is a mustard called shotweed (*Cardamine hirsuta*). Its ripe seedpods shoot seeds all over the ground. In other parts of the country, shotweed is called pepperweed, or bitter cress. To complete her salad, Pitcher mixes marmalade and vinegar for a vinaigrette dressing. "The taste complements the tangy wild greens."

At her Farm Wife Mystery School outside Seattle, Patti Pitcher teaches classes about foraging and storing wild edibles.

PATTI'S NETTLE SOUP

4 cups sliced potatoes

1 cup water

2 leeks (chopped)

1 small onion (chopped)

1 clove garlic (minced)

2 tablespoons butter

2 quarts chicken broth

½ pound nettles (leaves and tender tips)

½ cup heavy cream

1 teaspoon salt

¼ teaspoon black pepper

¼ teaspoon freshly ground nutmeg

1. Put potatoes and water into a soup pot, and cover with a tightly fitting lid. Bring to a boil, and cook until the potatoes are soft.

2. In another pan, sauté the leeks, onions, and garlic in the butter until all are soft. Add to the potatoes.

3. Once the potatoes are soft, add the chicken broth and heat until the mixture is simmering. Add the nettles and cook until very soft.

4. Pour a few cups at a time into a blender or food processor to blend the mix. Don't overdo it or the potatoes will get gummy. Once the mixture is blended, add the cream and spices.

When foraging for wild plants, always wear clothing and gloves—even in warm weather—to protect your body from stings and bites, scratches, sunburn, and poisonous plants. For extra protection, wear insect repellent and sunscreen as well.

Another weed in Pitcher's garden is stinging nettle (*Urtica dioica*). The leaves and stems are covered with tiny stinging hairs, so she uses garden clippers to harvest them. Once cooked, they don't sting. Nettles are delicious when sautéed with butter and garlic, says Pitcher, and they also make a tasty soup. Some people drink nettle water to ward off colds. To make nettle water, simply boil nettles in a pan of water, strain out the nettles, and save the water. Mixed with honey, nettle water helps soothe coughs. People claim that nettle water is good as a hair tonic, too, for preventing hair loss and dandruff.

BEFORE YOU PICK A PLANT

Picking and eating weeds and wild plants can be fun, and it's a great way to expand your menu. Keep in mind that some wild plants should *not* be picked because they are rare or endangered. Others are inedible or even poisonous. Here are a few pointers on harvesting edible plants. Before going out, be sure to do your homework. Invite an adult who can help you identify plants that are safe to eat.

1. **Wear clothing that will protect you from sun, insect bites, and plant irritants.** Use an insect repellent to discourage mosquitoes and ticks, watch out for stickers, and avoid picking plants in an area infested with poison ivy, poison oak, or poison sumac—or wear gloves.

2. **Be positive about plant identification.** Double-check field guides, online references, and apps to make sure you're harvesting a nutritious weed and not a poisonous look-alike. Wild plants have numerous common names, so stick with botanical names to eliminate dangerous confusion. For example, common purslane goes by many names, including duckweed and pusley. While purslane (*Portulaca oleracea*) is edible, the Florida pusley (*Richardia scabra*) is not.

3. **Don't harvest or eat wild mushrooms unless you are an expert.** Just don't. Many mushrooms are deadly.

4. **Harvest wild edible plants from safe places such as these:**
   - yards and gardens where you know they haven't been exposed to chemical poisons
   - uphill from roadways, avoiding areas downhill from roads and ditches where contamination from runoff collects
   - away from industrial and polluted areas

WHAT'S IN A NAME?

A few key terms are useful in understanding how a plant or animal fits into a local environment and into the local food chain.

INDIGENOUS (OR NATIVE) SPECIES: An *indigenous*, or native, species is one that originates and occurs naturally in a specific location.

INTRODUCED SPECIES: A species is *introduced* if it has been brought into a new location or ecosystem with human help. This can be accidental, as when insects bore into the wood of shipping crates, or deliberate, as when people put non-native plants into their gardens or import exotic pets. Many introduced species do not thrive or spread widely in the new location because the weather, soil conditions, and rainfall do not match the species' natural habitat.

INVASIVE SPECIES: An introduced species is *invasive* when it establishes an ongoing population and spreads beyond the area where it first arrived. It causes—or is likely to cause—damage in its new environment. This harm may be economic, as when a plant takes over and damages local crops, houses, and other property or clogs the waters in fisheries. The damage can be ecological. For example, an invasive plant or animal may do better than local species, outcompeting them for limited resources and causing them to die out. An invasive fungus or insect can even endanger human health by carrying or causing disease.

PEST: A *pest* is an organism that damages property, interferes with economic activities such as agriculture and forestry, or is harmful to the health of humans or domestic animals. A species that is a pest in one place may not be a pest in another.

5. **When harvesting greens and other wild salad ingredients from urban areas, check with a local university agricultural extension office, state environmental protection department, or regional Environmental Protection Agency (EPA) office for results of any testing on local soils or plants.** You can find contact information for these government offices in your area online. Definitely avoid plants from soils with high levels of lead or other contaminants.

6. **Before picking plants from a neighbor's property, make sure to get permission.** The same is true if you want to harvest from parks and other public property. A good place to start is by calling the city or county clerk's office about local parks, or checking your state department of parks' website. Contact information may be listed for individual parks. Keep in mind that some plants are protected species and it's against the law to pick them.

7. **Be environmentally responsible.** If you are harvesting native species, pick only about one in twenty plants, leaving enough to maintain the plant population. And take only what you will use. With invasive plants, pick as much as you want. But keep in mind that some invasive plants will spread if you leave bits of root or rhizome (underground stem) in the soil. Look online or in the library, and learn the best way to harvest without causing specific invasive plants to spread.

CHAPTER 2
PUT SOME WILD IN YOUR SALAD

EARLY COLONISTS TO THE AMERICAS WERE UNSURE OF THE FOODS THEY WOULD FIND IN THEIR NEW HOMES. So before they left Europe, they packed seeds from mustards, dandelions, and other plants from their homelands. They planted them in their new communities. Many of these plants, introduced to the American continent by the colonists, were so successful that they still cover the landscape.

Americans of later centuries came to consider many of these plants weeds. But before the plants became known as weeds, they were considered food. First Lady Martha Washington, for example, prepared purslane for George's dinners. Until the end of the nineteenth century, cooks and homemakers could easily find recipes for purslane and other traditional greens. But when farmers shifted from hand labor to mechanized agriculture, people changed the way they viewed these plants. Machines were unable to easily harvest purslane and certain other greens. Some grew too close to the ground for machine harvesting, and the machinery damaged others. So Americans began to think of them as unwanted weeds. Recipes for these healthy vegetable greens eventually disappeared from US cookbooks. Twenty-first-century Americans are interested in locally grown foods, and some are turning back to purslane and other weedy wild greens.

Mount Vernon, the estate where George and Martha Washington lived in Virginia, still maintains gardens of flowers and edible plants. Small gardens outside kitchens were common for centuries, and cooks relied on the produce for their menus.

PLEASE DO EAT THE DANDELIONS

Dandelions grow just about anywhere there is soil and sunlight. They are among the healthiest plants to toss into the salad bowl because their leaves are high in calcium, vitamin C, iron, and vitamin A. They've become so trendy that upscale food markets sell dandelion greens and dandelion tea.

Nearly every part of the dandelion is edible: leaves, flowers, flower buds, and roots. You can even eat the seeds, if you have the patience to separate the tiny seeds from their fluffy white parachutes. Dandelion leaves can be eaten raw in salads or sandwiches. They are especially good in egg salad sandwiches. The best time to harvest dandelion leaves is in early spring when they are small and tender. Make sure to pick leaves before the dandelion begins flowering because they get bitter as the plant matures. Leaves also become bitter in hot weather when it rains less often, so look for plants growing in wet, shady spots.

You can cook dandelion greens too—especially the larger leaves. Try steaming, boiling, or stir-frying them. You can sauté them with (or without)

Put petals in salads, fry in fritters and tempura, and add to bread and pie crusts.

Sprout seeds as you would alfalfa or other small seeds; add to cookies.

Add fresh greens to salads or sandwiches. Steam them for a healthy side dish. Add to soup, or use as a pizza topping.

Roast roots and grind them for a coffeelike drink.

bacon and add them to potato salad, quiche, or casseroles in place of spinach or kale. Cooks also blanch dandelion greens by boiling them in water for about five minutes and then plunging them immediately into icy water so the greens don't continue to cook. The quick cooking sweetens the greens, and the ice bath helps them keep their color.

Dandelion flowers make a sweet addition to cookies, cupcakes, biscuits, and bread. Some cooks even roll them into tortilla dough or sprinkle them over salad. What looks like one big yellow dandelion flower is actually a cluster of thin individual flowers. Each large head holds up to one hundred flowers. Each flower produces a seed, which means a single plant produces more than one thousand seeds over the summer. The trick to separating the individual flowers from the flower head is to hold the tips of the yellow flowers between the thumb and fingers of one hand and to pinch the green base with the thumb and fingers of the other hand. Then tug to release the flowers from the flower head.

DANDELION FLOWER PANCAKES

For a fresh take on pancakes, add some flower power. Collect a bunch of dandelion flower heads, and separate the flowers. To do this, hold the tips of the yellow flowers with the fingers of one hand. Then pinch the green flower base between the thumb and fingers of the other hand. Pull apart to release the flowers into a bowl.

2 cups flour

2 teaspoons baking powder

pinch of salt

1 tablespoon sugar

pinch of cinnamon

2 eggs

1½ to 2 cups milk

2 tablespoons butter, melted

1 cup dandelion flowers

Butter or vegetable oil for the griddle

1. Mix flour, baking powder, salt, sugar, and cinnamon together in a large bowl.

2. In another bowl, beat together eggs, milk, and melted butter.

3. Gently stir the egg mixture into the dry ingredients. If the consistency is too thick, add a little more milk, but not so much that it becomes too runny.

4. Fold in the dandelion flowers. They will make the batter a little thicker, and that's okay.

5. Put enough butter or vegetable oil on the griddle to coat its surface lightly. Heat at medium temperature. Ladle ¼ cup of pancake batter onto griddle. If it is too thick to spread on its own, use a spoon to spread it so it is about ¼ inch thick. If the griddle has enough space for another pancake, add another ¼ cup of the batter. Cook the cakes until golden on one side, then flip and cook until the other side is golden.

Makes about 8 pancakes. Eat them with syrup, honey, or jam.

Some people dip entire dandelion flower heads in cornmeal batter and fry them as fritters. As for the roots, people roast and then grind them to make dandelion root tea.

PLANTAIN PIZZA AND MORE

Plantains (*Plantago* spp.) are as hardy as dandelions and nearly as widespread. Common broad leaf plantain (*Plantago major*) has fat, spoon-shaped leaves that taste like nutty asparagus. Narrowleaf plantain (*P. lanceolata*) has thinner, lance-like leaves with parallel ribs (lines running from the base of the leaf to its tip). As settlers expanded westward in North America, plantain followed, earning the nickname "white man's footprint." Like dandelions, plantains are a good source of vitamin C and calcium. Use tender, young leaves for salads and sandwiches. Older leaves, chopped and boiled, make a good pizza topping.

Chickweed is another introduced species commonly found in lawns and gardens. The dainty leaves and stems are tender and mild. For a burst of green freshness, substitute them for sprouts in salads and sandwiches. Some people include chickweed as an ingredient when making pesto, or they steam entire plants just as they would steam spinach.

Lamb's-quarter stays tender and mild all summer. The leaves are naturally covered in a protective powdery coating of dried mineral salts that make them look dusty. Lamb's-quarter leaves, commonly called wild spinach, have a mild flavor and are perfect for recipes that would normally call for spinach. Include them in omelets and frittatas, lasagna and pasta, quiche, soups, and stir-fries. These plants are full of nutrients, and high in calcium and vitamins C and A.

Lamb's-quarter is also known as goosefoot, for the triangular webbed-foot shape of its leaves. Some people call it pigweed, which is confusing because there is another edible plant also called pigweed (*Amaranthus retroflexus*). Like lamb's-quarter, young pigweed leaves are mild and taste fine raw or cooked. Lamb's-quarter and pigweed are both members of the amaranth family and are native to the Americas. Knowing the scientific name is helpful to distinguish one plant from the other, but as far as eating goes, they can be used interchangeably.

Lamb's-quarter is considered a weed because it can quickly take over spaces with bare soil. Yet it is an extremely nutritious green because it has high levels of protein, calcium, phosphorus, iron, vitamin C, and vitamin A.

Both lamb's-quarter and pigweed produce edible seeds—a single plant can produce anywhere from thirty thousand to seventy-five thousand! Seeds can be cooked alone as cereal, added to oatmeal or rice, or tossed into the batter for muffins and breads. Sprouted seeds make tasty salad or sandwich toppers. You can even pop them! Heat a dry skillet over medium-high heat, and pour in about ¹/₈ cup of seeds. Shake the pan as the seeds pop (they won't pop very high). In twenty to thirty seconds, they will be ready to eat. Popped pigweed and lamb's-quarter seeds are much too small to eat as a movie snack, but they taste yummy sprinkled over yogurt and cereal.

WILD AND WEEDY QUICHE

4 to 8 slices cooked bacon (for a truly wild dish, use bacon from a wild boar, or substitute toasted or sautéed insects of your choice)

1 cup chopped onion

1 tablespoon butter or olive oil

1 cup canned or fresh tomato, peeled and chopped

pinch of thyme

pinch of oregano

salt and pepper, to taste

3 eggs

1 cup milk

½ cup grated Parmesan cheese

1 cup grated swiss cheese or a mix of ½ cup grated swiss and ½ cup grated cheddar

1 premade pie crust (8 inches, or 20 cm)

2 large tomatoes, sliced (for the crust)

1 cup cooked greens (lamb's-quarter, dandelion, or other wild green)

1. Fry the bacon in a large frying pan and set aside on a plate with paper towels to absorb any grease.

2. In a separate frying pan, sauté the onions in butter or olive oil for a couple of minutes. Add chopped tomatoes and thyme, oregano, and salt and pepper to taste. Cover and simmer for 5 minutes.

3. Uncover and mash the tomatoes and onion with a fork. Cover again and cook until the mixture becomes thick, about 5 minutes. Set aside to cool.

4. Meanwhile, beat the eggs and milk together in a large bowl. Stir in the grated cheeses. Then add the cooled tomato-onion mixture, and stir to blend all the ingredients.

5. Place the pie crust in an 8-inch (20 cm) tin pie dish (or use the pan the crust came in). Line the bottom of the pie crust with sliced tomatoes. Layer on the cooked bacon (or bugs) and cooked greens. Pour egg and cheese mixture over the top.

6. If you use a premade crust that comes in its own baking dish, place it on a baking sheet before putting it in the oven.

7. Bake at 350°F (180°C) for 30 minutes, or until a knife inserted into the center comes out clean. Before serving, allow the quiche to sit for about 5 to 10 minutes to set.

PICK A PECK OF PICKLED PURSLANE

Remember the purslane that George Washington ate? It's easy to spot. With succulent light green leaves and red stems, it looks almost like a jade plant. Its chubby water-filled leaves help purslane survive drought. Purslane even puts up with salt, making it perfectly adapted to city life in places where people use salt to melt ice on roadways and sidewalks.

Purslane tastes tart and peppery, like a lemony cross between spinach and watercress. Young leaves and stem tips make a juicy addition to green salad, potato salad, and sandwiches. They're also good steamed, stir-fried, pickled, added to stews and gumbos as a thickener, baked into casseroles, cooked with eggs, pureed into fruit smoothies, and sprinkled over pizza before serving. Purslane has more calcium, iron, and potassium than lettuce.

The flowers of the chicory plant (*Cichorium intybus*) are bright blue. The leaves look similar to dandelion leaves, and they alternate along their stems, which can grow up to 4 feet (1.2 m) high. Though edible, the leaves are bitter when raw, so blanch them before eating them. Some people brew roasted ground chicory root to make New Orleans coffee, a drink Louisianans invented when they could not get real coffee during the Civil War (1861–1865).

Curly dock (*Rumex crispus*) is a member of the buckwheat family. It grows in fields, vacant lots, and along roadways and is most noticeable when it goes to seed. That's when you see its tall stem topped with clusters of dark seeds. Curly dock gets its name from the curly edges on its leaves. The leaves make a good side dish when sautéed in olive oil with a tiny bit of garlic or onion. Dock leaves tend to be bitter so use just a few at a time. Try adding them to stir-fries, egg dishes, soups, and stews.

Red clover (*Trifolium pratense*) is grown as a hay crop for animal feed. It also grows in fields, yards, and along roadsides. The flowers look like pink pom-poms topping the plant. They are yummy when tossed raw into salads or cooked rice. You can also add a few blossoms to your tea the next time you make a cup.

Impress your friends! Host a pick-your-own salad bar and pizza-topping party.

PICKLED PURSLANE

This easy recipe is a version of refrigerator pickles.

- ½ cup white vinegar or apple cider vinegar
- 2 tablespoons white sugar
- ½ teaspoon salt
- ¼ cup cold water
- 1 cup of purslane

1. In a small nonmetal bowl, combine vinegar with sugar, salt, and water with a whisk or a fork.
2. Add the purslane.
3. Soak for at least two hours in the refrigerator before serving.

Purslane is native to India and Persia (what is now Iran) and has spread as an invasive weed throughout the world. Wonder what to do with it if it's spreading in your garden? Try eating it!

CHAPTER 3
EAT THE PUSHY INVASIVE PLANTS

LIKE EARLIER MIGRANTS, MODERN FAMILIES SOMETIMES CARRY SEEDS OF THEIR FAVORITE PLANTS WITH THEM WHEN THEY MOVE TO A NEW PLACE. When they plant the seeds, sometimes the introduced plants go rogue, escaping over the garden fence. Other plants arrive uninvited. Their seeds might cling to a traveler's clothes or shoes, or they may hitch a ride along with a ship's cargo or ballast water (water a ship carries to maintain balance and stability while sailing). The seeds may come with birdseed mix or travel in bags of potting soil or garden seeds.

When introduced plants spread aggressively, they compete with native species for sunlight, water, and space to grow. Estimates vary, but biologists have so far determined that up to 20 percent of introduced plants around the world are invasive and threaten biological diversity in the habitats to which they have been introduced.

Climate change also influences how—and whether—invasive plants expand their ranges. For example, warmer temperatures year-round and the arrival of earlier springs can give quick-blooming invaders an edge over slower-blooming natives, points out Elizabeth Wolkovich. She is an ecologist at the Biodiversity Research Centre at the University of British Columbia

Invasive plants, such as these kudzu vines, threaten biological diversity. Because they grow so aggressively, the plants hog sunlight and water and space, forcing out native species. Biological diversity is key to the health of any ecosystem. Kudzu leaves and flowers are edible!

in Vancouver, Canada. When invasives bloom earlier than native plants, they capture the lion's share of nutrients, water, and light, making it more difficult for native species to thrive.

THE PLANT THAT ATE THE SOUTH

Kudzu (*Pueraria montana*) has blanketed the American South, pushing its way into fields and forests, covering everything in its path. This vining member of the pea family is native to China and Japan, where it has been used for centuries as a food and fiber crop. Kudzu first came to the United States as part of the Japanese exhibition of the 1876 Centennial Exposition in Philadelphia, Pennsylvania. By the end of the century, southern gardeners were importing kudzu seeds and planting the ornamental vine to shade their porches.

In the 1930s, the USDA gave kudzu plants to southern landowners, hoping to reduce soil erosion caused by poor farming practices and deforestation. The agency even offered farmers an incentive of eight dollars an acre to plant kudzu. The USDA told farmers that kudzu plants would add nitrogen to improve the soil, and that it was good for livestock to eat and for making hay.

WILD KUDZU SALSA

1 cup kudzu vine tips, boiled and then diced

1 large tomato, diced

1 tablespoon minced onion

1 teaspoon olive oil

pinch of salt

2 tablespoons honey

1 tablespoon chopped cilantro or parsley

1 tablespoon lime juice

In a medium bowl, mix everything together and chill for a couple of hours. This salsa is good with your favorite corn chips or as a garnish for a pork roast or for baked or grilled chicken or fish.

What they didn't realize was that kudzu grew *too well*. During the heat of summer, kudzu vines can grow 1 foot (0.3 m) per day, extending their reach 60 feet (18 m) over a single season. The vines smother trees and other plants in their path under a thick mat of leaves. By 1953 the USDA had stopped promoting kudzu because of its invasive tendencies. However, kudzu continues to expand its range, crowding out native plants and interfering with farming across the South. And as Earth's climate warms, northern states are becoming warmer and more hospitable to kudzu. The invader is showing up in Massachusetts, New York, and parts of southern Ontario, Canada.

A creative way to deal with kudzu? Eat it! Kudzu leaves, gathered when the plant is young, can be served in salads, steamed as greens, or baked into quiche. Kudzu leaves are big so they also work perfectly as sandwich wraps. You can boil or bake kudzu roots just as you would potatoes. As for the flowers, they are fragrant and smell something like grapes. They can be batter-fried, dried for tea, or steeped in hot water to impart their flavor to jelly.

When foraging for kudzu in the wild, pay attention to the surrounding vegetation. Poison ivy may grow in the same habitat, and because both plants have three leaflets, they can be confused. But the petioles (leaf stems) of kudzu plants are covered with tiny hairs, while poison ivy petioles are smooth. Also, kudzu has purple flowers that grow in a showy cluster as long as 8 inches (20 cm). Poison ivy flowers are tiny, with green or white petals that form a star, and yellow centers. Just remember: When in doubt, don't eat it. And if you're harvesting edibles in poison ivy territory, wearing gloves is a good idea.

BEAUTY GONE BEASTLY

Japanese knotweed (*Fallopia japonica*), native to Japan, China, and the Korean peninsula, was introduced to the United States in the late nineteenth century. Gardeners liked its heart-shaped leaves, sprays of tiny white flowers, and tall, sturdy bamboo-like stems. Americans started planting Japanese knotweed for landscaping as well as for erosion control.

Japanese knotweed can grow up to 6.5 feet (2 m) tall and 65 feet (20 m) wide. Its shallow roots force their way through cracks in patios and concrete walkways, and into walls and floors. They can be very difficult to manage, so think before you plant them. However, if you find them in the wild, they are edible.

Like kudzu, Japanese knotweed spreads quickly, forming dense thickets that shade and squeeze out native plants. Since the year 2000, the International Union for Conservation of Nature (IUCN) has maintained a list of the world's worst invasive species. Japanese knotweed is so aggressive that it has made the top one hundred on the list, known as the Global Invasive Species Database. In wet areas, Japanese knotweed takes over stream banks, crowding out trees that provide vital shade for fish and wildlife. It turns out that knotweed isn't good for erosion control either. Its roots grow too shallow to hold down soil, and the plant dies back in the fall. That leaves stream banks more susceptible to erosion, not less.

SESAME KNOTWEED

8 cups young Japanese knotweed stalks, cut into pieces 3 to 6 inches (8 to 15 cm) long

3 tablespoons tamari or other soy sauce

1 tablespoon chili paste or ¼ teaspoon ground cayenne pepper (or to taste)

6 cloves of garlic, peeled and crushed

6 tablespoons raw sesame seeds

a small frying pan (cast iron works well)

1 cup cooked rice or your favorite ramen or other noodle

In a heavy saucepan or cast-iron skillet, mix knotweed, tamari or other soy sauce, chili paste or cayenne pepper, and garlic. Cover and cook on low heat until tender, about 20 minutes. Meanwhile, toast the sesame seeds.

So what is redeeming about this invasive? You guessed it. Its tender young shoots are crunchy and tasty—tart, like rhubarb. Some people simply clean, slice, and toss them into a salad. Others prefer Japanese knotweed shoots grilled, stir-fried, sautéed, pickled, or baked into pie with strawberries.

The best time to harvest Japanese knotweed shoots is early spring, when they first poke out of the ground. Don't worry about overharvesting, but do be sure to pick the entire plant, including all the roots. This plant regrows from the tiniest bit of rhizome, so be sure not to leave any behind in the ground, or even lying on the ground.

To Toast Sesame Seeds:

1. Place a small frying pan on medium-low heat. Do not add oil or butter; toasting works in a dry pan.

2. Add the sesame seeds right away.

3. As the seeds warm, gently shake the pan or stir the seeds with a wooden spoon so they are exposed evenly to the heat.

4. The seeds will turn brown and release a subtle, nutty aroma when they are done. This will take about 3 to 5 minutes.

5. Pour the seeds into a small bowl or plate so they can cool a little before you use them for garnish. If you don't use them all at once, you can store them in the refrigerator in a small jar with a lid.

Serve the knotweed over the rice or your favorite noodles. Sprinkle with the toasted sesame seeds.

STOVETOP FRITTATA WITH WILD GARLIC MUSTARD

1 tablespoon olive oil or butter

1/2 onion, peeled and chopped

1/4 cup sweet bell pepper, seeded and chopped

1/2 tomato, chopped

1 teaspoon thyme

salt and pepper, to taste

1/2 cup garlic mustard greens, coarsely chopped

4 eggs, beaten

1/2 cup grated cheese such as cheddar, Gouda,
   or Monterey Jack (optional)

1. Heat olive oil or butter in a large cast-iron skillet over medium heat. Sauté the onion until translucent, about 5 minutes.

2. Add chopped pepper, tomato, thyme, and salt and pepper. Mash the tomato with a fork, and continue cooking another 5 minutes, or until the tomato dries up a little.

3. Toss in garlic mustard greens, and allow them to wilt. This will happen fairly quickly, in 3 to 4 minutes.

4. Add eggs and sprinkle cheese on top. Cover and cook for about 8 to 10 minutes on medium-low heat until the eggs are set and the cheese has melted.

INTO THE WOODS

European colonists brought garlic mustard (*Alliaria petiolata*) to North America for food. They also mashed the roots to make poultices (pastes) for colds and bronchitis. Garlic mustard flowers have four petals, and the seeds of the plant are in slender pods. The leaves usually have a garlicky flavor, though this depends on the plant's maturity and location. The leaves of plants in shaded areas tend to be very mild, and the leaves of older plants tend to become bitter. The entire plant is edible. The greens are delicious in stir-fries, frittatas, soups, and stews. You can also add finely chopped garlic mustard leaves to mashed potatoes, biscuit and tortilla dough, or as an ingredient in pesto. Raw leaves and flowers go well in salads and sandwiches but should be eaten in moderation. Some cooks grate the roots and mix them with mayonnaise to make a dip resembling horseradish sauce.

PLEASE, EAT THE INVADERS!

Don't worry about picking too many garlic mustard plants. And feel free to yank them out by the roots. These plants are such aggressive invaders in northern forests that it's almost impossible to stop them from spreading. For example, a single garlic mustard plant can produce thousands of seeds, which remain viable in the soil for five years or longer. Once established, these plants tend to dominate the forest floor, spreading 20 to 120 feet (6 to 37 m) in a year. Deer don't like the taste of garlic mustard, so they avoid them, which also facilitates their spread.

Garlic mustard engages in chemical warfare against native plants. The mustard roots produce chemicals that harm mycorrhizal fungi in the soil. Those fungi live in a symbiotic (helpful and interdependent) relationship with the roots of trees and other forest plants. The fungi help the other plants absorb nutrients from the soil. Without the fungi, fewer trees grow and the trees produce fewer leaves. This affects salamanders and other species that make their homes in the leaf litter, the layer of dead leaves on the forest floor. To control garlic mustard, conservation groups organize trail hikes and weed festivals where volunteers harvest garlic mustard by the bushel. So please, eat the garlic mustard! And the kudzu and the Japanese knotweed. Be an invasivore (invasives eater) pioneer. Eating invasive plants won't eliminate them, but it can help control them.

DON'T BE A PATHWAY: STOP THE SPREAD OF INVASIVE SPECIES

To help stop the spread of invasive species, you can be a citizen scientist. Study field guides and reputable websites to learn how to identify invasive species of plants, insects, and other animals. Websites of university agricultural extension services and state environmental departments are a great place to start online. Once you know how to identify invasives, you can help out by reporting your sightings to your state's invasive species council, if you have one, or online at iMapInvasives or EDDMapS. Field agents can follow up on your information, perhaps with programs to control the invasive species.

Here are three basic tips for battling invasive species:

- If you are planting a garden, grow native plants, especially those that will attract butterflies, bees, and other pollinators and that will also benefit birds. If you already have invasive plants in your garden, dig them up so they won't spread. And eat them if they're edible!

- Never release exotic pets, domestic animals, live bait, or aquarium fish into the wild or into your community.

- Don't carry invasive species of any kind into a new area. For example, before planning campfires, check to see if there are state restrictions on

Bees are key pollinators of flowering plants, including edible species. When you plant a garden, include native species that attract pollinators.

transporting firewood, which may contain invasive insects. After boating, fishing, or hiking, clean your boat, trailer, and boots before going to another place. This step ensures that you won't transport organisms from one place to another.

POLLINATION BETWEEN FLOWERING PLANTS OF THE SAME SPECIES

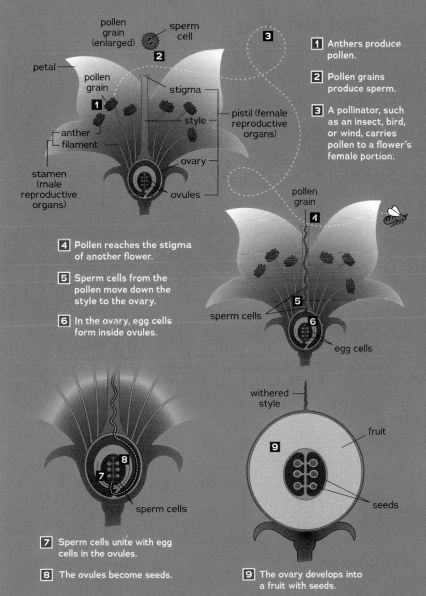

pollen grain (enlarged)

2 sperm cell

3

pollen grain

petal

1 pollen grain

stigma

style

anther

filament

pistil (female reproductive organs)

stamen (male reproductive organs)

ovary

ovules

1 Anthers produce pollen.

2 Pollen grains produce sperm.

3 A pollinator, such as an insect, bird, or wind, carries pollen to a flower's female portion.

pollen grain

4

5

sperm cells

6

egg cells

4 Pollen reaches the stigma of another flower.

5 Sperm cells from the pollen move down the style to the ovary.

6 In the ovary, egg cells form inside ovules.

8

7

sperm cells

withered style

fruit

9

seeds

7 Sperm cells unite with egg cells in the ovules.

8 The ovules become seeds.

9 The ovary develops into a fruit with seeds.

Three-fourths of Earth's flowering plants and about 35 percent of all food crops require animal pollinators to reproduce. These pollinators include bees, butterflies, moths, beetles, birds, and bats.

CHAPTER 4
EXOTIC PESTS CAN BE DELICIOUS

ANIMALS ARE ON THE MOVE. They're crawling, scampering, and hitchhiking across the continents. They're fluttering and flying through the air, and swimming or catching rides through oceans, rivers, and lakes. Sometimes they migrate on their own. Often they are carried to new homes by that most mobile of species—human beings.

Many animals don't survive in new habitats. But sometimes an introduced animal succeeds so well in a new ecosystem that it becomes invasive. For example, without natural predators, an introduced animal may outcompete native species. An invasive herbivore (plant eater) might overgraze, causing shortages of the native plants that local animals need for food or shelter. Invasive animals also sometimes bring new diseases to which native species have no immunity (natural defenses). The native species may begin to die off, sometimes to the point of extinction.

Humans sometimes relocate animals for what seem, at the time, to be good reasons. For example, when colonizing Australia, European settlers brought food animals with them. In the nineteenth century, they imported European rabbits (*Oryctolagus cuniculus*) to Australia for hunting. The bunnies multiplied like . . . well, rabbits . . . and before long Australia was overrun. By 1920 Australia's population of European rabbits grew to an estimated ten billion, causing widespread environmental damage and the extinction of native Australian species.

The feral pig population in the United States numbers between five and six million animals in at least thirty-five states. They adapt easily to new environments because they have no natural predators, are extremely fertile, and like to eat almost anything.

Invaders often receive unintentional human assistance in making their move. Insects and other critters stow away on ships, airplanes, cars, and trucks and hide out in suitcases. Fish and other animals raised for food may escape from their enclosures. Earth's changing climate has also created more opportunities for invaders to expand their ranges. For example, over the last few decades, warmer winters in the United States have allowed feral (wild) pigs to spread farther and farther north. During their sixteenth-century explorations, Europeans brought domestic pigs to the Americas as a food source. In the twenty-first century, descendants of those pigs run wild through at least thirty-five states. They trample woodland habitats, displace native species, and destroy farm crops and fences.

TALE OF A TASTY INVADER

Once established, invasive species can damage local environments and economies. Lake Victoria, Africa's largest lake, lies along the borders of Tanzania, Uganda, and Kenya. It was once home to up to five hundred species of native

A young woman in Kenya carries home a Nile perch from Lake Victoria. The species is Africa's largest freshwater fish, and it can reach 6 feet (1.8 m) in length.

fish. Around the 1950s, English colonial officials introduced the Nile perch (*Lates niloticus*) to Lake Victoria. They said the perch were large and good to eat, would provide good sport for European anglers, and would benefit commercial fisheries.

The Nile perch is, however, an aggressive predator that can grow up to 6 feet (1.8 m) long. The perch began to feed on smaller fish species in Lake Victoria. Within thirty years, more than two hundred of the lake's native fish species were extinct. Those smaller fish, which ate algae, had played an important role in the lake's ecology. Without them, algae levels soared, using up much of the lake's oxygen and creating dead zones where most fish couldn't survive. Lake Victoria became choked with weeds.

Meanwhile, businesses built factories to process Nile perch for export overseas. Many people profited from this new industry. At the same time, some local residents who had previously fished and eaten the native fishes, and small-scale fishing businesses that had relied on those species, suffered. And starting in around 2000, the Nile perch population declined, pushed lower by water pollution, lower oxygen levels, and overfishing. Because so many people have come to depend on the introduced Nile perch for their livelihoods, regional and international organizations are working together to manage the lake's health and bring back the perch. By improving water quality, these restoration projects may even help the remaining native fish populations begin to recover.

BUT ARE THEY GOOD TO EAT?

When unfamiliar animals show up in new places, local people may not recognize them as food. This is true even when invasive species are valued as tasty treats in the lands from which they originate. Iguanas, for example, are reptiles that are part of the traditional cuisine in their native habitats in Central and South America. Beginning in the 1960s, they invaded parts of the southern mainland United States, as well as Hawaii and Puerto Rico. In these places, however, many people think eating iguana is bizarre.

The common green iguana is an example of an exotic pet that has become an invasive pest. Some people buy them as pets and then discard them when they become unmanageable. To be part of the solution, avoid exotic pets altogether. Or try them as a menu item. They are popular in some parts of the world.

HOLY IGUANA!

Traditionally, many Roman Catholics refrain from eating meat on Fridays during Lent (the six-week period before Easter). On those days, they avoid the flesh of warm-blooded animals but may eat cold-blooded animals such as fish or reptiles. As a result, in some nations, Catholics customarily eat iguana on meatless Fridays. For example, iguana soup—made with the meat of the animal's tail and eggs—is a favorite Lenten meal in the Central American nation of Nicaragua.

The iguanas now living in Puerto Rico, Hawaii, Florida, and Texas are primarily common green iguanas (*Iguana iguana*), Mexican spiny-tails (*Ctenosaura pectinata*), and black spiny-tails (*Ctenosaura similis*). Biologists think that some of them arrived as stowaways on cargo ships carrying shipments of fruit from South America. Others probably started out as cute little pets that escaped from their owners' homes or grew too big and were released. Some of these reptiles grow up to 6 feet (1.8 m) long. Voracious feeders, they eat their way through suburban gardens, parks, and farmers' fields, munching trees, shrubs, flowers, and fruit. They also dig burrows beside or beneath sea walls, sidewalks, and foundations, weakening these structures.

In Florida the green iguana has helped cause the near extinction of a small butterfly, the Miami blue (*Cyclargus thomasi bethunebakeri*). The invasive iguanas eat the shoots and leaves of the gray nickerbean (*Caesalpinia bonduc*), an important host plant for the Miami blue butterfly. The butterfly lays its eggs on the native nickerbean bushes, and the caterpillars hatch there and eat the nickerbean leaves. When a caterpillar grows large enough, it forms a pupa, which is protected by a chrysalis. An adult butterfly emerges from the chrysalis, completing the insect's metamorphosis (transformation). In some areas where green iguanas have invaded, however, the butterflies cannot find enough nickerbean bushes. In addition, some biologists fear that the iguanas are eating the butterfly eggs on nickerbean leaves.

Tilapia is a popular fish in markets around the United States. They are an invasive species that many Americans love to eat.

Adventurous hunters in southern states have addressed the iguana problem by bagging the rampaging iguanas. Some of these hunters learned to love the taste of iguana meat. Why let it go to waste? Iguana fans fry the meat for tacos or spaghetti sauce. They say it is delicate and tender, and that it tastes like . . . chicken.

THE INVASIVORE MOVEMENT

In the early twenty-first century, forward-thinking chefs and environmentalists began to call for more invasivorism—eating invasive species. Invasivorism, they said, could help rid ecosystems of destructive pests. It could also provide low-cost, nutritious food for people. Harvesting invasive species requires fewer resources—such as water and food and human labor—than raising livestock for meat. Invasivores point out that, in addition, the meat of many invasive animals is tasty, wholesome, and free of the antibiotics and growth hormones that farmers often give to domestic meat animals.

Many Americans are already eating invasive fish—without realizing it! For example, markets and grocery stores throughout the United States sell tilapia at fish counters. Tilapia refers to a large group of mild-tasting white fish that are native to the Middle East and Africa. They are easy to raise in aquaculture operations, or fish farms. North American fish farms began raising tilapia in the 1980s. But many of the fish escaped, and they have become invasive in North American waters.

Other less familiar invasive animals include fish such as lionfish and Asian carp; mammals such as wild pigs and nutria; and marine species such as periwinkles. Why not try some? You may also want to learn more about pestarians, people who follow a mostly vegetarian diet that includes meat from pest animals.

"EXTINCTION IS A HAPPY ENDING"

Professor Joe Roman is a conservation biologist who teaches at the University of Vermont. He has been considering the benefits of invasivorism since the early twenty-first century. When he first floated the idea in magazine articles in 2004 and 2006, he was greeted with a great deal of silence. Americans thought invasivorism was too odd to take seriously.

Roman and his Eat the Invaders project set up a website providing information, recipes, resources, and encouragement for invasivores and would-be invasivores. He finds people have become more interested in knowing where their food comes from. They understand the advantages of eating local food. They want to eat for their own health and for the health of the planet. And it turns out that eating invasive species ties in nicely with those goals.

How effective can the Eat the Invaders campaign be? Roman points to the passenger pigeon (*Ectopistes migratorius*) as an example of a food species that humans wiped out. These birds were once one of the most common birds on Earth. Experts estimate the birds numbered in the billions. In the early nineteenth century, dense flocks of passenger pigeons darkened the skies of the eastern United States. A single flock could take two hours to pass overhead. They were easy to hunt, and they were a cheap, flavorful food. Pigeon pie was a popular dish throughout the United States. But by the beginning of the twentieth century, recreational and commercial hunters had killed so many that not a single wild passenger pigeon was left.

This illustration of passenger pigeons appeared in William B. Merson's 1907 book *The Passenger Pigeon*. Seven years after the book was published, the world's last passenger pigeon died. Scientists estimate that North America was once home to about five billion passenger pigeons.

Passenger pigeons were not an invasive species, and their extinction was a loss to the North American ecosystem. In contrast, biologists say there's no need to worry about overharvesting invasive species. In fact, Roman points out that eliminating an invader can actually help restore ecosystems and native species. He says that when it comes to invasive animals in a non-native ecosystem, "extinction is a happy ending."

CHAPTER 5
EXPAND YOUR AQUATIC MENU

WATER COVERS MOST OF EARTH'S SURFACE, AND MANY AQUATIC ANIMALS CAN THEREFORE EASILY MOVE LONG DISTANCES. With climate change, the ocean is becoming warmer. Pollution and lower oxygen levels are killing off certain marine species that other ocean creatures feed on. In response to these changing ocean conditions, some marine life-forms are moving.

The Pacific Ocean range of the jumbo squid, or Humboldt squid (*Dosidicus gigas*), for example, once centered close to the equator, from Chile to Southern California. Beginning in the 1980s, however, this squid expanded its range northward, reaching Canada and Alaska in about 2004. The jumbo squid is a major predator. Its growing presence in northern waters worries the fishing industry there, which relies on the fish that the squid eats. On the other hand, as the squid has become more common along the California coast, anglers have discovered the sport of squid fishing, and local restaurants are serving delicious jumbo squid dishes.

Other aquatic animals have landed in hospitable new habitats with a helping hand from humans. Wildlife officials and private landowners intentionally stock waterways with exotic fish such as Nile perch, in hopes of providing good fishing. Many organisms travel unseen in ballast water, carried in the tanks of large ships. Others hitch rides on boat hulls. Canals, built to connect rivers, lakes, and seas, also provide new routes for aquatic animals.

With climate change, many species are expanding their range. This scuba diver admires a jumbo squid at night in the Sea of Cortez (also known as the Gulf of California) off the coast of western Mexico. The squid's range now extends as far north as Alaska, where ocean waters have become warmer.

LIONFISH: DEADLY AND DELICIOUS

One appetizing invader is the lionfish, which is native to the reefs and rocky outcrops of the South Pacific and Indian Oceans. Two very similar species, the red lionfish (*Pterois volitans*) and the common lionfish (*Pterois miles*), have spread to Caribbean and southeastern US coastal waters. Lionfish, with their colorful red, white, and gold stripes and fancy, feathery fins, are popular additions to saltwater aquariums. But these beauties are predators, and they sport dangerous spines. Each fish generally has eighteen spines that can release venom—a toxic substance—when touched. Lionfish stings can cause intense pain and blistering, nausea, vomiting, and even seizures.

According to the US National Oceanic and Atmospheric Administration (NOAA), lionfish most likely arrived in the Caribbean Sea, Gulf of Mexico, and Atlantic Ocean along the Florida coast in the 1990s. NOAA says aquarium owners probably threw a few unwanted lionfish into the ocean. Others speculate that in 1992, Hurricane Andrew damaged a Florida fish tank, releasing several lionfish.

Ships sailing across the sea and through rivers and canals into the Great Lakes are the primary source of invasive species in that lake system. Ships leaving port without a full load of cargo fill large onboard ballast tanks with local water, to improve balance and stability. This water can contain thousands of stowaways—from microscopic plankton to large schools of fish. The ships empty their tanks when they take on cargo at other ports—releasing these organisms into waters far from their origin.

That's how the pesky zebra mussel, *Dreissena polymorpha*, arrived in the Great Lakes from eastern Europe and western Russia in the 1980s. The zebra mussel—a small, striped bivalve (a soft-bodied aquatic animal in a shell with two hinged halves)—has spread rapidly in the United States. Zebra mussels attach themselves to firm objects, including boats, fishing lines, docks, and the inside of pipes. They clog boat motors and block intake pipes for water treatment plants, power plants, and irrigation systems. They eat microscopic plants and animals, consuming so much that native fish and wildlife are starved out. They cause increased algal blooms (rapid algae growth) in lakes and rivers, and they smother native mussels. Zebra mussels are not a safe food choice for invasivores, however, because their tissues can accumulate toxic substances from polluted water.

These bilingual signs at a boat launch ramp at Lake Mead near Las Vegas, Nevada, warn against transporting invasive mussels.

The US Fish and Wildlife Conservation Commission promotes eating lionfish. The fish are such a popular menu item that restaurants can't keep up. Many people like eating an invasive species as a way to help the environment. In 2015 the program Seafood Watch named lionfish a green option. That means it's a great choice for sustainable seafood. If you live in Florida, check out the nearest Whole Foods store in your neighborhood. They sell lionfish!

Regardless, lionfish spread quickly. Away from their native habitat, they have no natural predators. Their fearsome spines protect them, and they reproduce rapidly. Lionfish are most troublesome among the coral reefs of the Florida coast and Caribbean Sea, where their population has exploded. They eat huge numbers of native reef-dwelling fish such as parrotfish and wrasses. The lionfish invasion has reduced the numbers of native fishes by up to 80 percent in some areas and has caused widespread damage to delicate reef ecosystems.

Many government agencies concerned with the health of the reefs have tried to control lionfish. This fish's spines make it challenging to catch, but divers use nets or spears to do the job safely. Because lionfish meat is delicious—white, flaky, and delicate—one major goal around the Caribbean region has been putting lionfish on local dinner plates.

At first, most people in the United States and in Caribbean nations declined to catch or eat the lionfish. So in 2009, the government of Jamaica established the National Lionfish Pilot Project. It included an education campaign urging, Let's Eat It to Beat It. It worked.

HOW TO CLEAN A LIONFISH

Cleaning a lionfish is much like cleaning any other fresh fish. However, it is especially important to remove the spines as you clean and prepare the fish. Many cooks and fishers offer easy online tutorials for cleaning, scaling, gutting, and filleting fresh fish. Check YouTube or start with the URLs below. Here's how chefs prepare a lionfish for cooking.

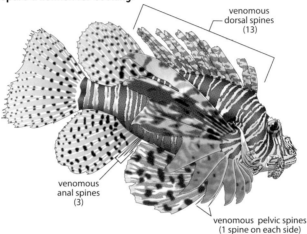

venomous dorsal spines (13)

venomous anal spines (3)

venomous pelvic spines (1 spine on each side)

Directions:

1. Wear kitchen gloves when working with a lionfish. Not everyone does, but it is a smart safety step to avoid a puncture.

2. Use a pair of kitchen shears to remove all the spines by cutting above or into the flesh along each side.

3. To dispose of the spines, wrap them in thick layers of paper first.

4. Scale and gut the fish, using a sharp kitchen knife. To see how a chef does this with a fresh black bass, check out this URL: https://www.youtube.com/watch?v=ZiGEN2F_spc.

5. Then cut the fish from the tail to the head.

6. The next step is to fillet the fish. See how the chef does it with a fresh black bass at this URL: https://www.youtube.com/watch?v=TBBkRTPSgtA.

7. The fish is then ready to cook, whether by baking, grilling, or poaching.

Jamaican spearfishers stepped up efforts to catch lionfish. Shoppers beg. buying lionfish steaks at markets. By 2014 Jamaica's National Environment and Planning Agency was reporting a significant drop in the number of lionfish in areas of intense fishing. Researchers anticipate this will allow native reef fish populations to recover, at least in some areas.

The Florida Fish and Wildlife Conservation Commission also promotes eating lionfish. In fact, lionfish has become such a popular menu item from Florida to New York that restaurants can't always meet the demand. People love the taste, and they also like the idea that by eating this invasive fish they can help the environment. In 2015 Seafood Watch, a respected program that rates seafood based on whether it is fished or farmed in ways that maintain healthy oceans, named lionfish a green option. That means it's a "Best Choice" for sustainable seafood. The lionfish listing sparked interest among some grocery chains. Whole Foods Market, for example, began buying lionfish from divers and training store personnel to handle the fish safely. The market is also selling lionfish fillets in Florida stores.

It is clear that spearfishers alone cannot catch enough fish to meet the demand for lionfish fillets. Further, although many lionfish live near the ocean surface, many more live hundreds of feet below, beyond the reach of spearfishing divers. Scientists and government agencies, including the Office of National Marine Sanctuaries (part of NOAA), are working to develop lionfish-specific traps that can catch the spiny invaders in deeper waters. They hope these traps will help move more lionfish out of the reefs and onto the table.

WHAT'S A WINKLE?

Invaders don't have to be big or fierce to disrupt ecosystems. The common periwinkle, *Littorina littorea*, is a small sea snail with a grayish shell. Periwinkles are native to the Atlantic coasts of Europe, including England—where "winkles" are a traditional seaside snack. Fish-and-chips shops sell fried winkles in paper bags or piled high in newspaper cones, sprinkled with vinegar or salt. To eat them, people suck the meat straight from the shell or pull it out with a toothpick. They may also dip the winkle meat into mayonnaise, melted butter with garlic, or another favorite sauce.

HIGH TIDE, LOW TIDE

Along the seacoast, water levels rise and fall in relation to the land, in a pattern of high and low tides. The tides are caused by the gravitational pull of the moon and the sun on Earth as Earth rotates. On the side of Earth closer to the moon, the moon's gravity pulls the ocean water toward the moon. It takes just over six hours for the water to move from high tide to low tide, so that in a twenty-four-hour period, there are usually two high tides and two low tides. The water level along the shore can vary by 3 feet (1 m) or more in height. The intertidal zone, the area that is covered by water during high tides and uncovered during low tides, is home to a rich diversity of plants and animals. Among these are crabs, sponges, sea stars, anemones, jellyfish, algae, eelgrass, and seaweed (not all of which are edible).

Periwinkles migrated across the Atlantic Ocean from Europe to the states of New England in the mid-nineteenth century, probably hitchhiking on ships. From Long Island Sound (New York) northward to Nova Scotia (Canada), they have become the most common sea snail on the northeastern coast of North America. They have displaced some native populations of sea snails.

Periwinkles have drastically altered North American shorelines. In the intertidal zone—the shore between high tide and low tide—the periwinkle scours everything down to bare rock. It uses its file-like tongue to scrape off algae, plants, and the jellylike eggs of native sea snails and other small aquatic animals. This scraping makes beaches bare. It can destroy Atlantic coast salt marshes, the intertidal wetlands regularly flooded and drained by ocean tides. Salt marshes are important in controlling coastal erosion. They are also valuable habitat for a rich range of plants and animals, including shrimp, crab, and fish.

Enter the invasivores! In the early twenty-first century, conservation biologist Joe Roman was studying the ecology of Atlantic shorelines. The extensive damage done by periwinkles worried him. One day, as he collected crab samples on a beach in Nova Scotia, he saw a man gathering periwinkles. At first, he assumed this fellow collector was a biologist. But the local beachcomber explained that, in fact, he sold the snails to New York restaurants.

The light bulb went off for Roman. What if we ate the invaders? After all, he recalled, his Italian great-grandmother had gathered periwinkles on Rockaway Beach, in New York City, to add to her homemade pasta sauce for Sunday dinners. The result of Roman's brainstorm? The Eat the Invaders project, whose motto is "Fighting invasive species, one bite at a time." Roman is the "editor 'n' chef" for the organization.

As part of his teaching at the University of Vermont, Roman organizes a formal dinner for students in his marine ecology course. A local chef prepares the menu, which features dishes made with invasive seafood. Roman's students are often skeptical when faced with periwinkles in the shell.

Professor Joe Roman organizes a popular meal each year at the University of Vermont, where he teaches marine ecology. The entire menu focuses on invasive fish species, and students love it!

PASTA AND PERIWINKLES

Try this special dish, based on Joe Roman's great-grandmother's Sunday spaghetti sauce recipe. It's perfect after a day of beachcombing and gathering periwinkles. This dish is best prepared from freshly gathered local periwinkles. If you can't collect them on the beach yourself, you might be able to purchase them at a specialty fish market in your area.

(With thanks to Joe Roman and http://eattheinvaders.org/.)

2 cups of periwinkles in their shells

½ teaspoon salt, plus salt and pepper to taste

1 tablespoon olive oil

3 cloves garlic, peeled and chopped

1 teaspoon fresh chopped or dried parsley

**3 cups fresh, or 1 can (20 ounces) plum
     tomatoes, chopped**

1 pound dry spaghetti

Italian bread

½ cup Parmesan cheese, grated

1. Wash fresh periwinkles thoroughly in cold water.

2. Add periwinkles to a large pot of boiling water with a small handful of salt. (The salt helps shrink the meat and makes it easier to remove.)

"I was definitely nervous when I saw them," Jordyn Chace, a member of Roman's class, confessed after one dinner. "I have never eaten anything like them before." But Jordyn realized the periwinkles "smelled great," and she reported that after dipping them in warm butter, she was ready to pop them in her mouth. The taste made Jordyn a convert. "I ended up going back for

3. Boil uncovered for 3 to 5 minutes. The snails are ready when the operculum—the "lid" across the opening of the shell—falls off.

4. Remove from heat, drain, rinse the periwinkles in cold water, and let them sit for about 10 minutes to cool.

5. When cool to the touch, remove the periwinkles from their shells with a toothpick, pin, chopstick, or small fork. (Recruit some helpers. This step takes some time.) Set them aside in a small bowl.

6. Add olive oil to a large skillet over medium heat. Then sauté garlic in oil until golden, about 2 or 3 minutes. Add chopped parsley and tomatoes. Add salt and pepper to taste. Cook at medium-low heat for about 15 minutes.

7. Meanwhile, boil water in a soup kettle and add spaghetti to the water, as directed on the package.

8. After you add the spaghetti to the water, add the periwinkles to the sauce.

9. Put the cooked and drained spaghetti into a large bowl. Add the tomato and periwinkle sauce, and stir to blend.

10. Serve hot, with crusty Italian bread and grated Parmesan cheese.

seconds and thirds," she said. Roman's marine ecology students are willing to put periwinkles on their plates in part because they understand the importance of supporting native species and ecosystems. As Jordyn put it, "It also felt good knowing that by eating these snails I was helping in a small way to restore balance to the ecosystem."

MORE INCREDIBLE EDIBLES

Here's a selection of edible aquatic invasive species that have made their way to the United States. They may be invading a water body near you. If you can't catch your own, check out your local grocery store, food co-op, ethnic market, or specialty fish shop to see if they carry any of these species. If not, they may be able to help you find a place that does.

- **CHINESE MYSTERY SNAIL.** (*Bellamya chinensis*). This large freshwater snail was introduced to the United States in the late nineteenth century through Asian food markets and has spread from coast to coast. Some experts recommend cleansing the snails for several days in clean fresh water to flush out toxins before eating the snails.

- **EUROPEAN GREEN CRAB.** (*Carcinus maenas*). This small crab from Europe is one of the world's most successful invaders. It has established populations on both the East Coast and West Coast of the United States. It outcompetes native species and is reducing populations of native oysters, small fish, scallops, and crabs. Though small, the green crab makes good eating, particularly in its soft-shelled phase.

- **GIANT TIGER PRAWN.** (*Penaeus monodon*). This huge native of the Indian and Pacific Oceans has invaded the Gulf of Mexico. It is good

QUIT YOUR CARPING

The large and hungry Asian carp has spread through the Mississippi River system and is threatening to move into the Great Lakes. The Great Lakes, five huge interconnected lakes along the United States–Canada border, are a precious natural resource. Together they contain about 6 quadrillion gallons (23 quadrillion L) of fresh water, making up the largest freshwater system on Earth. The Great Lakes are home to more than 170 species of fish and are important to the economies of both the United States and Canada. They are also popular for recreational fishing and boating.

The so-called Asian carp is actually four different species of carp—bighead eating and is often raised for food. But it is an aggressive predator, and escapees have the potential to destroy native Gulf species.

- **NORTHERN SNAKEHEAD.** (*Channa argus*). This sharp-toothed predator is a native fish of China, Russia, and Korea. It can grow to 3 feet (0.9 m) in length. It was spotted in scattered locations in the United States beginning in the late 1990s. An established population in the Potomac River system in Maryland and Virginia is a potential problem for native species there. In its native range, the snakehead is a popular food, and people also use extracts from the fish to help heal wounds, including after surgery. Enjoy fillets of tender, mild snakehead grilled, baked, or fried.

- **PURPLE VARNISH CLAM.** (*Nuttalia obscurata*). A recent newcomer from Japan, this invader outcompetes native clams along the northwestern coast of North America. The purple varnish clam is tasty in chowder.

- **RED SWAMP CRAYFISH.** (*Procambarus clarkii*). Native to the southeastern United States, this crayfish is invasive elsewhere. Try crayfish steamed or boiled, whole or chopped in a salad.

carp (*Hypophthalmichthys nobilis*), black carp (*Mylopharyngodon piceus*), grass carp (*Ctenopharyngodon idella*), and silver carp (*Hypophthalmichthys molitrix*). They are all native to Europe and Asia. In the 1960s and 1970s, managers of sewage ponds and aquatic farms in the southern United States imported the carp. They believed the fish, which eat enormous amounts of algae and plankton, would keep their ponds clean.

But some carp escaped. And after flooding in the 1990s, large numbers of them moved into the rivers, lakes, and streams of the Mississippi River system. They traveled as far north as Minnesota, and experts fear they are poised to invade the Great Lakes.

Asian carp consume vast quantities of the algae and plankton that native fish depend on. They starve out other fish, and they outreproduce them too. A single female bighead carp, for example, can produce one million eggs in her lifetime. The adults are too large for native predators to eat. The result is that on some stretches of river, more than 90 percent of the biomass (living material) in the water is Asian carp. A widespread carp invasion in the Great Lakes would endanger the lakes' native plants and animals. It would also pose a serious risk to the commercial fishing industry and local economies of the Great Lakes region.

Silver carp pose another hazard too. In response to the noise of a boat's engine, these fish leap from the water. In an instant, the air can fill with flying

Silver carp jump out of the Illinois River near Havana, Illinois.

A sign warns boaters and barge operators that they are about to enter an electric fish barrier zone on the Chicago Sanitary and Ship Canal. The electric barrier is meant to keep the Asian carp from invading the Great Lakes. But a live Asian carp was caught beyond the barriers, just 9 miles (14 km) from Lake Michigan.

50-pound (23 kg) fish. As they leap and fall back into the water, they damage boats and injure boaters. They also land in the boats themselves! Invasivore Jackson Landers dubs them "the easiest fish to catch in North America."

In 2002, to prevent Asian carp from entering the Great Lakes, the US Army Corps of Engineers built the first of three electric barriers within the canal system that connects the Mississippi River system with the Great Lakes. The barriers are located in the Chicago Sanitary and Ship Canal in Romeoville, Illinois, about 37 miles (60 km) downstream from Lake Michigan. They send pulses of electricity through the water to discourage the fish from swimming past them toward the lakes. Experts are not certain the barriers will be 100 percent successful.

Landers and others see a cheaper, easier solution: Eat carp! Full of protein and healthy fats, carp is nutritious and tastes like other firm, white fish.

SUSTAINABLE SUSHI CHEF

Bun Lai is the chef and owner of Miya's Sushi in New Haven, Connecticut. Don't look for a California roll on his menu, though. This sushi chef is committed to using ingredients that are sustainable and local. For this reason, Lai doesn't offer common sushi selections such as bluefin tuna. Bluefin and other popular fishes have been overharvested from the world's oceans, and their numbers have plummeted.

Instead of fishes from far-off waters, Lai uses ingredients caught locally, many from nearby Long Island Sound. Working this way eliminates long-distance shipping and higher greenhouse gas emissions. The chef says it also allows him to return to sushi's roots, that is, "to use what we have available where we live."

An enthusiastic fisher and diver, Lai noticed that certain invasive species were overrunning local shell-fishing beds. He began harvesting and preparing these invasive species for his customers. The menu at Miya's Sushi features the Asian shore crab, for example. This predatory crab eats the larvae of many shellfish and has reduced the populations of native species in the Atlantic Ocean along the coast of the northeastern United States. By collecting and preparing the Asian shore crab for his restaurant, Lai is helping to reduce their numbers, hoping to give native species a chance to recover.

Lai also prefers to use ingredients that usually go to waste—like broccoli stems. His restaurant offers salads prepared from Maine and Connecticut seaweed. He makes dishes with local kelp and weeds that he and his staff forage. Japanese knotweed is a favorite ingredient. He also serves sushi rolls topped with dried or smoked insects, such as crickets and black soldier flies.

When Lai first started serving these unfamiliar foods in his restaurant, customers walked out. But he kept at it, and once people tasted his food, they came back. Miya's Sushi has become widely recognized for its creative cuisine and for encouraging people to think more about what they eat. In 2016 the Obama White House named Lai as one of its White House Champions of Change for his work supporting sustainable seafood.

Chef Bun Lai prepares *wabisabi* rolls made from Alaskan sockeye salmon and wild grape leaves that he foraged himself.

Chef Tim Creehan (*right*) and Chef Philippe Parola prepare carp at a Chicago high school. They were part of the launch of a campaign by the Illinois Department of Natural Resources to teach people how to cook the fish.

People in Asia love to eat carp. In fact, some businesses in the United States have begun to catch and export Asian carp back to Asian markets. Carp in Asia is often raised on fish farms or caught from polluted waters, so some say the American wild-caught carp is better tasting.

Many Americans, on the other hand, consider carp an undesirable fish, in part because of its many small bones, which are difficult to remove. Chef Philippe Parola of New Orleans, Louisiana, is working to increase the American appetite for carp. He has renamed carp "silverfin™" to help diners think of it as a welcome menu item instead of a trash fish. Chef Parola has developed better deboning techniques and bone-free recipes for carp such as fish cakes. Experts agree that Asian carp are so plentiful in US waters that there's no risk of overfishing them. Meanwhile, a vibrant market for fishing and eating carp can help control the booming carp population.

CHAPTER 6
LAND INVADERS ON YOUR PLATE

ONE OF THE MOST DESTRUCTIVE TERRESTRIAL (LAND-BASED) INVADERS TASTES JUST LIKE BACON. It's the wild pig! Europeans introduced pigs, or swine, to the Americas centuries ago. Spanish explorer Hernando DeSoto brought a dozen or so domesticated hogs (*Sus domesticus*, or *Sus scrofa domesticus*) with him when he landed in Florida in 1539. Pigs are hardy and reproduce quickly, so within three years, DeSoto's herd had grown to seven hundred or more.

DeSoto's expedition drove the pigs along as they traveled throughout the Southeast. Some of those swine strayed into the wilderness along the way. This was the start of the feral swine population in the American South. As the years went by, settlers coming to Virginia, New England, and beyond brought more pigs, and more got loose.

Later, starting in the twentieth century, American hunters introduced wild boars (*Sus scrofa*) from Europe and Asia for sport hunting. These "Russian boars" or "Eurasian boars" were first introduced in North Carolina and surrounding states. They are prized by hunters because they are intelligent and fierce—and also tasty. Wild boars, the ancestors of domesticated pigs, can grow up to 3.6 feet (1.1 m) tall and weigh up to 710 pounds (320 kg). They have long snouts; thick, bristly coats; and long, straight tails. (The domestic pig, in contrast, is known for its curly tail.)

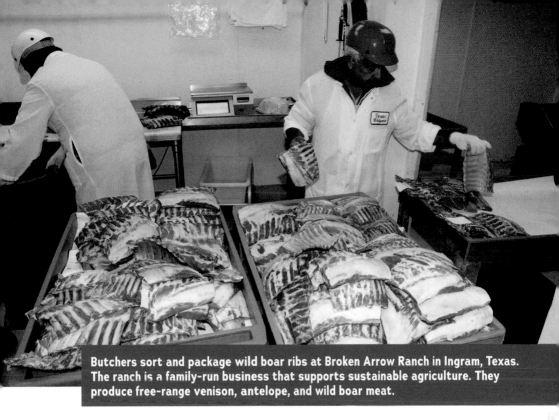

Butchers sort and package wild boar ribs at Broken Arrow Ranch in Ingram, Texas. The ranch is a family-run business that supports sustainable agriculture. They produce free-range venison, antelope, and wild boar meat.

Male wild boars grow long, curving tusks on both the upper and lower jaw. Females grow smaller tusks on the lower jaw.

Domestic pigs that escape and become feral adapt quickly to life off the farm. With each generation in the wild, feral pigs develop more characteristics of wild animals. For example, farmers typically trim the tusks of domestic pigs. In the wild, feral pig tusks grow up to 7 inches (18 cm) long. Feral pigs have interbred with the Eurasian boars initially imported for hunting. All these pigs in the wild are now referred to as wild or feral pigs, swine, hogs, or boars. The bristly ridge or mane along the back of the wild boar is the source of another well-known name for them: razorbacks.

In the centuries since DeSoto's landing, wild pigs have spread to more than thirty-five states. Subsequent settlers brought pigs to farms throughout the continent, and more escaped. Earth's warming climate has expanded the range where feral pigs can do well. Pigs are smart and adaptable. They are enthusiastic omnivores, eating almost anything, including the eggs of turtles, wild turkeys and quails, agricultural crops, fruits, nuts, acorns, and roots. They dig up to 3 feet

(0.9 m) deep when rooting for food. Large, aggressive, and destructive, they trample fields, create large craters when rooting for food, destroy crops and fences, and deplete other animals' food supplies. In 2015 the USDA estimated that feral pigs cause $1.5 billion worth of damage annually. These animals sometimes carry diseases such as swine brucellosis and tularemia, which they can transmit to domestic livestock, wildlife, pets, and people.

PUTTING WILD PORK ON THE PLATE

Federal, state, and local governments have spent millions of dollars to control the spread of wild pigs. One strategy is putting wild pork on people's plates. The meat is leaner (less fatty) than most pork from domesticated pigs, and some say it even tastes a little sweeter.

In many states, hunting the wily wild pigs is a popular pastime. Hunters who nab feral pigs can dress and cook them for their own use. To avoid the diseases that pigs can carry, anyone who handles these pigs is advised to wear rubber gloves. Wild pork can be prepared like domestic pork and used to make dishes including sausages, chili, pork chops, barbecued ribs, and bacon.

Landowners can also trap wild hogs alive and sell them for meat. To be sold commercially, however, animals must be slaughtered at a facility certified by the USDA. The certification is meant to ensure that the animal is treated properly and the meat is healthy to eat. In Texas, home to about half the nation's wild swine, the state has certified about one hundred buying stations where trappers can sell pigs they catch alive. The pigs are then shipped to approved slaughterhouses. This helps Texas ranchers and landowners turn their unwanted feral hogs into cash payments and get that tasty wild pork onto the plates of the public.

NUTRITIOUS NUTRIA

Nutria (*Myocastor coypus*) are beaver-like South American rodents with big orange teeth. The creatures, 2 to 3 feet (0.6 to 0.9 m) long, are semiaquatic, living partly on land and partly in the water. Beginning in the late nineteenth century, fur farmers imported nutria to many states, including California and

CHECK THE RULES

Before heading out to hunt or fish for any animal, check the rules in your state. Most states require you to have a hunting or fishing license. Game animals can generally be taken only within specific hunting seasons.

When it comes to invasive species, though, different regulations may apply. For example, Texas allows the hunting of feral hogs with the landowner's permission twenty-four hours a day, 7 days a week, 365 days a year, with no limit on the number of hogs taken. Similarly, the State of Florida has no limit on the number of lionfish that anglers can harvest in Florida waters. In other states, officials have limited or banned hunting pigs or other invasive animals to avoid encouraging people to release more invasives for hunters to pursue.

In addition, federal law prohibits importing or transporting "injurious wildlife" between states without a federal permit. Species defined as injurious, or harmful, include bighead carp, zebra mussels, Nile perch, and Burmese pythons.

Louisiana, to raise them for their luxurious fur. Nutria fur was very popular in the 1930s, but in later decades, it went out of fashion and fur prices declined. As fur farmers went out of business, they released their nutria. Many escaped into the swamps of Louisiana, particularly during hurricanes in the 1940s.

Also, in the 1940s, people intentionally introduced nutria to control weeds in coastal areas around the Gulf of Mexico. That proved to be a bad idea. Nutria destroy native plants, crops, and wetlands. Often called swamp rats, nutria outcompete the native muskrats. By the 1950s, the wild nutria population in Louisiana had swelled to an estimated twenty million animals.

Nutria have caused serious damage to the wetlands of Louisiana. They chew through the root systems of wetland plants. This destruction of vegetation leads to erosion of the low-lying swampy lands. The surface of the marsh sinks, and water floods in, converting valuable wetlands into open water. In addition, nutria burrows can cause severe erosion along riverbanks.

PYTHONS ON A PLATE? NOT THESE

Burmese pythons (*Python molurus bivittatus*) entered Florida as pet snakes. Some of them escaped or were released. These predatory snakes grow to more than 20 feet (6 m) in length. They have taken over wilderness areas of South Florida, where they have decimated local wildlife in the Everglades and surrounding areas.

Snakes are generally edible. But Florida officials warn residents not to eat the meat of these pythons. The Everglades ecosystem has heavy mercury contamination. Because the python eats other Everglades animals including alligators, which have high mercury levels, the toxin accumulates in the snake's tissues and is not healthy for humans to eat.

Although many snakes are edible, Burmese pythons are not safe to eat. They are prone to high levels of mercury contamination.

Nutria even dig holes in the levees (riverbank walls) that protect cities from floodwaters. They are, in short, a menace.

While nutria range from Maryland all the way to the West Coast, the largest populations are along the Gulf Coast. In New Orleans, nutria can be spotted poking their heads out of drainage canals and gutters. Although they look like overgrown rats, nutria are clean animals, eating only vegetation. In fact, according to the State of Louisiana, they are a healthy food choice, containing more protein and less fat than other meats.

Rural residents of Louisiana have been trapping and eating nutria for decades, and the state government has encouraged more people to give it a try. Nutria tastes similar to rabbit or dark turkey meat—but it's challenging to overcome many people's reluctance to eat rodents.

Nutria are common near waterways in Gulf Coast states of the United States—and can sometimes be found on dinner tables!

Stewed nutria may be enough excitement for some people. Adventurous eaters seeking more unusual fare might want to forage for snails or bullfrogs.

- Brown garden snail (*cornu aspersum*). This native of countries around the Mediterranean Sea is appreciated as a delicacy (escargot) in France. Brown garden snails have invaded parks and gardens across much of North America, damaging plants. You'll do local gardeners a favor if you collect bunches of them to eat. Try them fried in olive oil.

- Bullfrog (*Lithobates catesbeianus*) (*below*). Native to eastern North America, American bullfrogs are invasive outside their original range. They are widely farmed, and when they escape, they damage local ecosystems and contribute to the extinction of native frogs. Conservation biologists recommend catching your own bullfrogs west of the Rockies where they are invasive, rather than supporting bullfrog farming. Bullfrog legs are a delicacy. Try them Cajun-fried or with teriyaki sauce.

In the 1990s, Louisiana officials began working with New Orleans chef Philippe Parola, who is also known for his Asian carp recipes. Chef Parola created recipes and held nutria tastings and demonstrations to persuade restaurants to offer nutria dishes. The Louisiana Department of Wildlife and Fisheries posts recipes on its website, for dishes from nutria chili to nutria sausage to stuffed nutria hindquarters. It still isn't everyday fare for most people, but nutria meat is available in some Louisiana restaurants and online markets. As Chef Parola says, "More people are eating nutria than ever before."

CHAPTER 7
BUGS FOR LUNCH

IN 1875 CHARLES VALENTINE RILEY, MISSOURI'S STATE ENTOMOLOGIST—OR INSECT EXPERT—THREW A DINNER PARTY. He promised guests a four-course meal featuring local food. The invitation was welcome, because it came during a time of near famine. Thick clouds of Rocky Mountain locusts had swarmed across Missouri, gobbling everything in their path: crops, grass, stored grains, fruits—even the wool off of sheep. The insects descended across the land in masses so thick that people cleared them with shovels and fed them to their animals.

Riley knew that American Indians in the area roasted locusts for food, and he decided that other Missourians could turn the tables on these pests. He planned a menu of locust soup, baked locusts, locust cakes, and locusts with honey. His goals: to demonstrate that locusts were a good source of protein for hungry settlers and that the insects tasted good too. Some who took the challenge claimed the locusts tasted like crawfish. One local caterer even promised to put them on his menu.

Eating insects—or entomophagy—isn't as unusual as many North Americans believe. Nearly two billion people around the world are entomophagists. People from 80 percent of the world's cultures harvest—and eat—more than nineteen hundred different insect species. For example, deep-fried grasshoppers are a favorite treat in Mexico. In parts

Locusts swarm in Morondava, a town on the western coast of the island nation of Madagascar in the Indian Ocean. Locusts are an edible insect.

of Asia, Africa, Australia, and Central and South America, people snack on the larvae of wasps and other insects.

We may think eating bugs sounds gross, but that's just one point of view. In some parts of the world, people find the idea of peanut butter and jelly sandwiches equally revolting.

WHY EAT BUGS?

The main reason people eat insects is because they're delicious! Certain ants taste sweet and nutty. Some stinkbugs have an apple flavor. Grubs and worms taste like bacon. And remember those locusts the settlers ate in 1875? Right now, their cricket relatives are hitting store shelves in snack packs and protein bars.

Bugs have also been dubbed a superfood, a food that is high in nutritional content. When properly harvested and cleaned, insects are a very healthful food source, providing nearly the same levels of protein, vitamins, and minerals as fish, meat, and beans. And they're lower in saturated fats, the fats that increase the risk of heart disease and stroke.

When we say *bug* in this chapter, we're referring to many different kinds of arthropods. An arthropod is a creature with no internal skeleton. It has a hard outer exoskeleton, a body divided into segments, and jointed legs. Biologists have identified about one million species of arthropods. The arthropods are divided into different scientific categories. Some of them are listed here.

- **INSECTS**: Six-legged arthropods with three body parts (a head, a middle section called the thorax, and an abdomen), antennae, and compound eyes (made of many small units that work together). Most insects have one or two pairs of wings. Ants, beetles, and crickets are all insects.

cricket

- **TRUE BUGS**: A subgroup of insects with sucking mouthparts, including squash bugs, stinkbugs, and bedbugs.

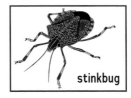

stinkbug

- **ARACHNIDS**: Eight-legged arthropods with two body parts (a cephalothorax—the combined head and thorax—and an abdomen). Unlike insects, arachnids have no wings or antennae. Spiders and scorpions are arachnids.

scorpion

- **MILLIPEDES AND CENTIPEDES**: Long, wormlike arthropods with many legs. Millipedes have two pairs of legs per body segment, while centipedes have one pair per segment.

millipede

- **SOW BUGS**: These little critters, sometimes called pill bugs, or roly-polies, roll into a ball when startled or touched. Like lobsters, crayfish, and barnacles, sow bugs are crustaceans. But because they're small and land-based, we think of them as bugs.

sow bug

A market in Oaxaca, Mexico, offers a range of edible insects. Raising insects is Earth-friendly, and the creatures are highly nutritious.

EAT INSECTS TO CONSERVE RESOURCES

Another reason for eating bugs is that it's good for the planet. That's because raising insects for food requires less land, water, and feed than raising cows, chickens, or pigs. So entomophagy can help save natural resources such as habitats for wild animals and plants, and clean water for humans and animals to drink.

Producing beef, chicken, and pork requires a great deal of real estate. Including the land devoted to pasture and crops to feed animals, nearly 70 percent of agricultural land in the United States is used for raising livestock. Around the world, jungles and forests are being cut down, in many cases to clear land for grazing animals. Edible insects, however, can be raised on tiny plots and in bins stacked on top of one another. Producing 1 pound (0.5 kg) of beef requires ten times the land area as producing 1 pound of edible cricket protein. Pound for pound, raising chickens or pigs takes nearly three times as much land as raising crickets. Eating more insect protein and less of other meats can help conserve

NUTRIENTS IN INSECTS AND OTHER MEAT

The USDA measures nutrients in food by the gram. This chart compares the nutrition provided by 100 grams of different insects and commonly consumed meats.

	Protein (g)	Fat (g)	Calcium (mg)	Iron (mg)
INSECTS				
Cricket	12.9	5.5	75.8	9.5
Giant water bug	19.8	8.3	43.5	13.6
Grasshopper	20.6	6.1	35.2	5
June beetle	13.4	1.4	22.6	6
Mealworm	2.7	5.4	23.1	2.2
Silkworm	9.6	5.6	41.7	1.8
FAMILIAR MEATS				
Chicken, skinless	21	3	12	1
Beef, 90 percent lean ground	26.1	11.7	13	2.7
Salmon, wild	19.8	6.3	12	0.8

land, including forested land. This is important because the world's forests play a key role in absorbing the carbon dioxide that fuels global warming and in producing the oxygen we breathe.

Raising insects for food also requires less water than raising other livestock. This is especially true when you consider the water used for growing the crops to feed the animals. To produce 1 pound (0.5 kg) of crickets, a grower needs about 1 gallon (3.8 L) of water. A single hen egg requires an average of more than 50 gallons (190 L) of water to produce, and 1 pound of beef takes close to 2,000 gallons (7,571 L)!

In addition, bugs have more efficient digestive systems than other farm animals. This means they are better at turning the food they eat into protein that

Data from Julieta Ramos-Elorduy, "Creepy Crawly Cuisine," *Food Insects Newsletter* 9, no. 2 (July 1996): 48–49; USDA National Nutrient Database for standard reference (ndb.nal.usda.gov/ndb/).

Magnesium (mg)	Potassium (mg)	Thiamin (mg)	Niacin (mg)
33.7	347	0.4	3.8
NA	NA	0.09	3.9
NA	NA	0.23	4.6
NA	NA	0.3	4
60.6	340	NA	5.6
49.8	316	0.12	0.86
25	229	NA	8.2
22	333	0.04	5.6
29	490	0.23	7.8

people can eat. For example, a beef cow converts only about 10 percent of the food it eats into edible protein. About 90 percent of what it eats goes to waste. In contrast, insects convert up to 90 percent of what they eat into edible protein.

EAT BUGS TO CLEAR THE AIR

Finally, raising insects instead of beef cattle can help reduce greenhouse gas emissions. Farming machinery used in growing feed crops and tending livestock produces carbon dioxide emissions. What's more, cattle themselves produce methane, which also contributes to global warming. Cows are ruminants, meaning their food goes through a digestive process called enteric fermentation. Microbes inside the cow's stomach break down fibrous grasses and grains,

COWS, CRICKETS, AND CARBON DIOXIDE

Raising livestock adds carbon dioxide (CO_2) to the atmosphere from emissions from farm machinery, vehicles that transport the animals to market, irrigation systems, and processing plants that are powered by fossil fuels. Historically, the EPA has tracked carbon dioxide emissions from all sources, including agriculture. Scientists collect data about the production of animal protein, including levels of greenhouse gases produced. They can then calculate how many grams of carbon dioxide are released for every kilogram of growth for different animals. This chart compares the grams of carbon dioxide produced per kilogram of growth for common livestock and three kinds of minilivestock (insects). **For reducing your carbon footprint, eating insects is a pretty effective choice!**

Cattle	2,850 g CO_2/kg growth
Pigs	80 g CO_2/kg growth
Locusts	18 g CO_2/kg growth
Mealworms	8 g CO_2/kg growth
Crickets	2 g CO_2/kg growth

producing methane. Cows expel the gas from their bodies. Methane absorbs far more heat than carbon dioxide, so it heats Earth even more. The US Environmental Protection Agency (EPA) has estimated that 1 ton (907 kg) of methane in the air absorbs twenty-eight to thirty-six times more energy from the sun than 1 ton of carbon dioxide. Many insects also release small amounts of greenhouse gases during their digestive processes. But insects aren't ruminants, and the amount of methane they produce, even when raised in large numbers, comes nowhere near the levels in cow manure, belches, and flatulence.

United Nations food experts believe that entomophagy can help feed a growing and hungry world population. The UN Food and Agriculture Organization (FAO) has been working since 2003 to promote edible insects as part of its efforts to fight global hunger. For example, FAO funds research into the benefits and challenges of entomophagy. It also works to educate and raise awareness of the advantages of eating insects. FAO brings together international experts in nutrition, farming, and government relations from the Netherlands to Africa, and from Asia to North America to help people raise insects for food.

BUGGY FOR CHOCOLATE

Just one more thing: you probably have already eaten bugs. Every time you devour a chocolate candy bar, chances are that you're eating bugs or at least bug parts. The US Food and Drug Administration (USFDA) publishes a guide for food manufacturers establishing how many insect parts are safe and acceptable in different foods. For example, the agency allows up to sixty bug bits in 100 grams (3.5 ounces) of candy bars. When it comes to peanut butter, thirty insect fragments or fewer are allowed per 100 grams.

Many manufactured foods have bug bits in them. For example, when you eat a chocolate candy bar, you are more than likely eating a small—and safe—amount of bugs.

USFDA regulators say that eliminating insect parts from our food is impossible. Using more insecticides to try to reduce the insects would put more toxic chemicals into our food. The risk isn't worth it. According to the USFDA, a few bugs in our food won't hurt us. Those insects are natural, unavoidable, and nonhazardous.

BEFORE YOU BAG A BUG

When diving into entomophagy, always know what you're eating. Here are some safety pointers:

When you first start exploring edible insects, including those that are packaged or prepared in restaurants,

- **No bugs for you if you have shellfish allergies.** People who are allergic to shellfish should avoid eating insects. Like insects, shellfish are arthropods—members of a huge and diverse biological phylum, or group. Insects and shellfish share common proteins that can cause allergic reactions in some people.
- **If you have another type of food allergy, start small with insects.** Eat very small portions to begin with. Invite an adult to be with you—and have your allergy remedies handy just in case you have a reaction.

When preparing insect-based meals,

- **Think about the sources.** Raise your own insects or buy them from a trusted insect farm or market to ensure that they are safe to eat. Animals, including insects, can absorb toxic chemicals into their tissues if they eat contaminated foods or live in polluted environments. Learning about the producers who raise edible insects can be a good way to determine which brands or markets provide healthful choices.
- **Clean and cook.** As with other meats, you should always wash your insects before cooking and cook them before eating them. You can roast, grill, boil, deep-fry, or toast them, depending on your recipes and your tastes.

For serious entomophagists who want to catch their own insects,

- **Know your insects.** Study before you start collecting insects on your own in the wild. Make sure you know which bugs are edible and how to identify them. Consult a reputable field guide, with illustrations, photos, or both. You can also look online, but stick to reliable resources such as a university's entomology (study of insects) department or an agricultural extension service. (Check Further Information at the back of this book.) See if adults in your family, school, neighborhood, or community can help you find edible insects. You'd be surprised that some adults enjoy edible bugs!

- **Red, orange, yellow: Avoid that fellow.** Pay attention to the colors of the insects you are thinking about eating. In the wild, bright colors such as red, orange, and yellow are a warning. They warn predators that an insect is unsafe to eat or even poisonous. Brown and green bugs are usually okay to eat. Even then, make sure you've properly identified the insect before eating it.

  Unless you have positively identified an insect as edible, avoid hairy insects whose hairs may irritate the mouth and throat. Avoid insects that spray a stinky liquid. (This is another of nature's warnings to stay away.) Stay away from insects that are known to eat poisonous plants such as poisonous mushrooms. And definitely don't eat insects that carry diseases, such as ticks and most mosquitoes.

- **Harvest clean insects from safe places.** Stick to yards and gardens that you know are not treated with pesticides or other chemical poisons. When collecting edible insects, stay away from industrialized and polluted areas. When collecting near roadways, avoid ditches where contamination from runoff collects. Keep to the uphill side of the road instead.

- **Wear clothing that will protect you from sun, insect bites, and plant irritants.** And remember to apply insect repellent to discourage mosquitoes and ticks.

CHAPTER 8
CRICKETS ARE THE GATEWAY BUG

BUGS ARE FINDING THEIR WAY ONTO OUR PLATES.
That is fine with actresses Salma Hayek and Shailene Woodley. Hayek loves fried ants and guacamole. Woodley, who has snacked on ants and June bugs, thinks insects are the "future of food." But if you are uncertain about swallowing wiggly critters—then good news! Crickets are for you. They are one of the most popular insects on dinner tables around the world because they are plentiful, nutritious, and easy to cook. Best of all, they don't wiggle. After enjoying their nutty flavor, many beginning entomophagists go on to try other insects, earning crickets the label of "gateway bug."

Crickets (family Gryllidae) live on every continent except Antarctica. They are easy to catch, and they are good eating. They absorb seasonings well, so chefs add onion, garlic, hot pepper, or soy sauce to their cricket dishes. Crickets can be fried, roasted, boiled, and toasted. They make crispy salad toppings and are fantastic in tacos. Some bakers add them to brownies and cookies.

Whole, deep-fried crickets are a treat in many countries, including Cambodia. Angelina Jolie, actress and UN goodwill ambassador, says munching a crunchy fried cricket is like eating "a potato chip." Jolie got hooked on crickets after she adopted a son from Cambodia. She wanted her children to appreciate Cambodian cuisine, and once she and the kids tasted crickets, the insects became a favorite family snack.

A tourist in Beijing, China, discusses his snack options with a vendor. Should he try a scorpion or a silkworm chrysalis on a stick?

Cricket powder, sometimes called cricket flour, is another great way to eat crickets. You can make your own by using a blender to grind roasted crickets into a powder. Cricket powder can be used like flour in baking. Crickets are gluten free, so people who want to reduce or eliminate gluten in their diet can enjoy baked goods made with cricket powder instead of wheat flour. Cricket powder is such a good source of protein that athletes stir it into their smoothies. A few companies manufacture high-protein snacks such as protein bars made with cricket flour. Some natural grocery stores, food co-ops, and sporting goods outlets stock cricket bars, but most sales are still over the Internet.

In many countries, people have eaten wild crickets, grasshoppers, locusts, and katydids for centuries. Sacred texts tell of people eating these insects long ago. For example, the Torah instructs Jews, "You may eat any kind of locust, katydid, cricket or grasshopper." Modern rabbis haven't officially certified crickets as kosher (meeting the requirements of Jewish dietary laws), but some Jewish people have argued that they should. The Christian gospels report that John the Baptist ate "locusts and wild honey" during his time in the desert. Islamic hadiths, texts of the

CRICKETS ARE THE GATEWAY BUG　　**83**

MORMON CRICKETS

The Mormon cricket, *Anabrus simplex*, isn't a cricket at all. It's a katydid. It was an important food source for the Paiute, the Ute, and other American Indians of the West. And it saved the day for the Mormon settlers in the late nineteenth century, when settlements in the Great Basin territory (which later became Utah) ran out of food. They lost their crops to drought and insect damage, so they turned to the local Ute people for help. The Ute shared their traditional prairie cakes with the settlers. The protein-rich cakes helped the Mormons survive the harsh winter. They loved the prairie cakes until they learned the cakes were made from berries, nuts, and . . . katydids. Though the food had saved their lives, the settlers refused to eat prairie cakes after that.

sayings of the Prophet Muhammad, say that Muslims may eat locusts because these insects "are the game of the sea."

In Mexico *chapulines*, or small grasshoppers, are a popular snack. People collect them in the countryside, then toast them on a griddle with oil, and season them with garlic and lemon or lime juice. In 2017 the Seattle Mariners baseball team introduced the snack to the concession stands at their home stadium. Baseball fans gobbled up the *chapulines* so fast that vendors sold out. A few weeks into the season, the team's concession stands had to set a limit on how many *chapulines* each fan could buy so there would be enough for everyone!

HOW TO CATCH A CRICKET

Online markets sell commercially raised crickets for human consumption. But if you want to go wild, here's how to catch your own:

- Crickets are nocturnal—they come out at night. They like to hide in dark places, so the trick to collecting them is to attract them to a dark place. Start by making cricket bait. Mix equal parts white sugar and bread crumbs. Use plain soft bread without spices, and start small, using one-half cup of each ingredient.
- Just before sunset, sprinkle the bread crumb bait over a small area in a garden or grassy outdoor spot. Cover the area with a sheet

Chapulines (small grasshoppers) are terrific toasted and seasoned with lemon and served in a warm tortilla. They are popular in Mexico—and at Seattle Mariners ball games!

of newspaper, and weight it down at the corners with rocks so it doesn't blow away.

- The next morning, go out early before the sun warms up your plot. Take a large jar and its lid with you. To check your cricket trap, lift the newspaper. If you see crickets, sweep them gently into the jar with your fingers. Don't be surprised to see ants and other sugar-loving insects hanging out under the newsprint. If you accidentally scoop up other bugs, you can separate them out later.
- Pop your fresh catch into the freezer for at least twenty minutes. Freezing is the most humane way to kill insects. Twenty minutes isn't long enough to kill crickets, but it does send them into a comalike state. Then the crickets are ready to use in cooking. Pour them into a colander and rinse them in cold water. Take out any bugs that aren't crickets, and toss the bugs outside for birds to eat.
- If you want to save your crickets to cook later, freeze them for an hour or two. Once they are frozen solid, separate out any unwanted bugs and pour the crickets into a plastic freezer bag for long-term storage. If you use a ziplock bag, it will be easy to add more frozen crickets as you collect them over time. Uncooked crickets can remain frozen like this while you collect enough for a recipe, but after a month in the freezer, they won't be as good to eat.

HOW TO COOK A CRICKET

Crickets that have been chilled in the freezer for twenty minutes and then rinsed are ready to be cooked. Use them for stir-frying, adding to stews and sauces, or substituting for meat in your favorite recipe. Thoroughly frozen crickets, however, need to be thawed before using.

To give their crickets a crunchy texture, many entomophagists roast or toast them, either to eat as snacks or to use in recipes. Crunchy crickets are great in salads, tacos, and as pizza toppers.

Some people boil the crickets before roasting, because it softens the hard exoskeleton and wings.

You can also give your crickets extra flavor by soaking them overnight in a marinade before roasting or toasting them.

To Boil Crickets (to Soften and Cook)

1. Fill a 2-quart saucepan halfway with water, and bring to a boil.

2. Place chilled crickets into a colander, and rinse them in cold water before putting them into the boiling water. Or, use frozen crickets after thawing.

3. Gently boil them for 5 minutes.

4. Drain the cooked crickets. They are ready to soak in the Secret Bug Sauce (see page 87) overnight or to use in other recipes.

To Roast Crickets

1. Preheat the oven to 225°F (110°C).

2. Spread about one 1 of crickets (boiled or frozen—not just chilled—and then thawed) on a lightly oiled cookie sheet. Bake until they are crisp—about 30 minutes—stirring occasionally. Test one (cool it first) to see if it is crunchy enough. If not, leave it in the oven for a few more minutes.

To Toast Crickets

Pan-toasting takes less time than roasting in the oven and is a good way to add crunch when all you've got is a grill, campfire, or stovetop. But it doesn't thoroughly cook the insects, so you must boil them first.

1. Toss one cup of boiled crickets in a lightly oiled cast-iron skillet.

2. Cook on medium heat for 6 to 8 minutes, shaking or stirring frequently so they don't burn.

3. Season with chili or curry powder—or just salt and pepper.

SECRET BUG SAUCE

Make ahead of time, and use as a marinade for crickets, beetles, grasshoppers, cicadas—even stinkbugs! The recipe was shared by Missouri entomophagist and master naturalist Paul Landkamer.

1/4 cup hot pepper sauce

1/4 cup soy (regular or tamari) or Worcestershire sauce

1/4 cup water

3/4 cup sugar

4 teaspoons garlic powder

1 teaspoon ground ginger

1 tablespoon cumin

1. In a large bowl, whisk together the sauces, water, sugar, and spices.

2. Place boiled insects in a bowl, and pour enough Secret Bug Sauce to cover them. Put them in the refrigerator overnight. Store unused sauce in a jar in the fridge.

3. The next day, drain crickets and roast or toast them.

TO FARM OR TO FORAGE?

Incorporating insect protein into our human diet requires more than foraging. Insects are plentiful in nature. However, some wild insects are contaminated with insecticides, lead, and other toxins. So we can't rely only on wild insects to provide food on a large scale. Farming insects offers a solution. Bug farmers can provide clean, safe, edible insects when they protect their minilivestock from pesticides, herbicides, and other pollutants. They can also produce a reliable, steady harvest of bugs every season.

Many insects are already raised commercially for nonfood purposes. For example, farmers in China and other parts of Asia have cultivated silkworms for centuries. To make silk fabric, manufacturers spin the silken threads the silkworms produce. Some people raise honeybees for their honey and as pollinators to help pollinate (fertilize) crops. Others raise cochineal insects for their carminic acid, a key ingredient in red dyes for food and cosmetics. And for organic farming, an entire business has grown around raising ladybugs and other beneficial insects. These bugs help farmers control insect pests without pesticides.

Cricket farming for food is widespread, at least in countries such as Thailand, Cambodia, and Vietnam. Family farmers usually set up low-tech ventures—small sheds in their yards where they breed and raise crickets. The baby crickets grow in plastic bowls or hollow logs or egg cartons. The farmers feed the crickets leftover scraps, such as pumpkin or other vegetables, rice, grass, flowers, or finely ground commercial chicken feed. Farmers protect their crickets from hungry ants by digging a ditch around the cricket rearing area and filling it with water and fish. Ants trapped in the moat end up as fish food. Farmed crickets are popular, and farmers report that some customers prefer the taste of farmed insects over that of wild-caught crickets.

In the United States and Canada, farmers have grown crickets for pet food for many years. But raising them for humans to eat is relatively new. And crickets destined for the dinner table must meet tough health regulations. Entrepreneurs have established cricket farms in several states, including Vermont, Montana, and Texas, as well as in Ontario, Canada. Raising crickets is not technologically complex. But to succeed, farmers must understand cricket biology, how to keep

Kyle Conrad raises crickets and other edible insects at Rocky Mountain Micro Ranch in Denver. It is Colorado's first and only edible insect farm, founded in 2015 by Wendy Lu McGill, an entomologist. The farm raises crickets, mealworms, and other edible insects for restaurants.

the insects healthy, how to assure good rates of reproduction, and how to avoid contamination from pollutants in the food or water supply. Cricket farmers are experimenting with different types of enclosures and methods to collect cricket eggs, feed and water the insects, and harvest adult crickets.

VISIT TO A TEXAS CRICKET FARM

If you're expecting gently rolling pastures, a big red barn, and cows grazing by the fences, think again. This farm, operated by the Aspire Food Group, sits in an industrial warehouse near the airport in Austin, Texas. Inside the warehouse, it's hot—close to 90°F (32°C)—and humid. About 50 percent humidity, says Jeanette Brown, the farm manager. The air is filled with nonstop chirping, like your backyard on a hot summer day—if you had a million crickets.

The cricket-rearing rooms are lined with shelves running from one end to the other, separated by aisles. Square plastic bins fill the shelves, each bin containing thousands of crickets. It's hard to get an exact count, Brown says. Crickets like dark spaces, so within each bin, thin cardboard or plastic dividers create a grid

CHIRPY-CHIP COOKIES

The quickest way to insect love is to toss roasted crickets into your favorite cookie or brownie recipe. Here's a chirpy take on chocolate chip cookies.

1 cup softened butter or margarine	1 teaspoon vanilla
$^1/_2$ cup granulated sugar	$2^1/_4$ cups flour
$^1/_2$ cup brown sugar	1 teaspoon baking soda
$^1/_2$ cup powdered instant milk	2 cups semisweet chocolate chips
2 eggs	$^1/_2$ cup roasted crickets

1. Preheat oven to 375°F (190°C).

2. In a large mixing bowl, blend butter or margarine, sugars, and powdered milk until smooth.

3. Beat in eggs and vanilla.

4. In a smaller bowl, sift together the flour and baking soda. Then stir into the mixture.

5. Stir in chocolate chips and crickets.

6. Drop rounded tablespoons of cookie dough onto ungreased baking sheets. Bake 9 to 11 minutes. Cool on baking sheets for 2 minutes before moving to cooling racks.

of small cells. Set across the top of the dividers are flat plates filled with organic grains. A watering station, with an upside-down plastic bottle on a dish, is set at the top of each stack.

Brown points out, "If the temperature and humidity are right [the crickets are] happy to stay in the bins." So she and her workers don't need to cover the bins with lids or screens.

Adult crickets at the Rocky Mountain Micro Ranch in Denver live in and on eggshell-style cardboard.

Newly hatched crickets, called nymphs, look like tiny, less developed adults. Because they are growing quickly, they need more water than adults during the first two weeks of life, Brown explains. The cricket farmers used to walk between the stacks, feeding crickets many times a day. Now a robot rolls down the aisles dispensing the proper amounts of food into each bin. Sensors in the bins monitor every aspect of the crickets' lives. That data is used to predict nutritional needs for the cricket herd. Automation and artificial intelligence fit well with Aspire's mission, which is "to farm insects that have the protein quality of meat and an environmental footprint like plants."

Under ideal conditions, it takes about one month to raise a cricket from hatch to harvest. During that time, the growing cricket will molt—shed its hard exoskeleton, or outer skin—about eight times. The farmers time their harvest to collect the crickets before the final molt. That way, Brown says, the exoskeleton won't be too tough to nibble. This cricket farm harvests hundreds of thousands of crickets each day.

One of the perks of being a cricket farmer is that Brown can take crickets home to use in her own cooking. "I've used whole crickets in tacos," she says. "They taste a little like crunchy chicken skin, and they're pretty good in salads, too."

CHAPTER 9
RUSTLE UP SOME GRUBS

GRUBS GET NO RESPECT. The truth is they taste good, once you get over their appearance. Grubs look like fat, white worms. They are actually the larvae of insects—usually beetles but sometimes moths. What grubs lack in crunch, they make up for in chewiness. And unlike crickets, they don't jump, skitter, or fly away when you try to catch them.

Beetle larvae are thinner-skinned than their parents. They don't have wings, so they move more slowly and are therefore easier to catch than adults. Beetle larvae live in soil, rotting logs, and even in the pantry. If you unearth a bunch of old, outdated granola bars stashed way in the back of a top shelf, don't be surprised to find some tiny grubs when you peel off the wrapper. These are probably the larvae of *Tenebrio molitor,* a darkling beetle. These grubs are also called mealworms. Like crickets, mealworms are also raised commercially as food for reptiles, birds, and other pets.

People have discovered that mealworms are yummy when fried in potato pancakes, sautéed in spaghetti sauce, baked in cookies, and tossed on top of pizzas. Mealworms taste a bit like nutty shrimp. Some growers feed the larvae chopped fruit rinds or grated carrots for a day or two before harvesting, to give them a sweeter taste.

Weevils are beetles with long noses. Palm weevil larvae (*Rhynchophorus* spp.) are a popular food in tropical regions. Palm weevils lay eggs inside holes they bore into the trunks of palm trees. When the eggs hatch, the weevil larvae

Life cycle of the darkling beetle

egg

larva
(mealworm)

pupa

adult

This infographic illustrates the complete metamorphosis of the darkling beetle, from egg to adult beetle. The larvae (known as grubs or mealworms) are a popular, edible treat in many parts of the world.

burrow through the tree, feeding on the palm wood. In Thailand grub farmers raise palm weevil grubs in large plastic buckets. Families stir-fry the grubs, add them to curry dishes, or dip them in batter and then deep-fry them.

Mopane worms are fat and meaty. They aren't worms at all. They are the larvae, or caterpillars, of an emperor moth (*Gonimbrasia belina*). They live in the African countries of Zimbabwe, Botswana, Namibia, and South Africa, where they spend their youth munching the leaves of the mopane tree. The caterpillars sometimes become pests, getting so abundant that their weight bends tree limbs. Harvesting them for food not only fills the pantry but also provides chemical-free pest control. After people collect the mopane worms, they gently squeeze them—to get rid of poop in the gut. Then they boil the larvae in salted water and dry them in the sun before storing. Shriveled and gray, they may not look appetizing, but once they are rinsed and boiled, they plump right up. A popular dish in the southern African region is to mix some dried mopane worms with chopped onions, peppers, tomatoes, and curry powder, simmer it all in a skillet on the stove until done, and spoon the yummy morsels over cooked rice or on other grains.

FRIED GREEN TOMATO HORNWORMS

Americans don't usually eat grubs. But some gardeners are open to the idea when the local larvae population grows to pest levels. Curious cultivators who want to avoid chemical pesticides may test some home recipes with wiggly ingredients from their gardens. It's pest control with benefits. Tomato hornworms (*Manduca quinquemaculata*) are a good place to start. These are hawkmoth caterpillars that devour leaves of tomato, eggplant, and pepper plants.

Hornworms eat the leaves of tomato plants. But the larvae will also eat eggplant, pepper, and potato plants. Hornworms are tasty in soups and stews!

They grow as long as 4 inches (10 cm) and taste like green tomatoes. Chefs say the best way to cook them is to fry them, but not for too long because they'll lose their color and might pop open. People also boil and dry them or roast them. Hornworms make meaty additions to soups and stews.

Those bright green cabbageworms (*Pieris rapae*) and the loopers (*Trichoplusia ni*) that feast on cabbage and broccoli make great additions to stir-fries. So do armyworms (*Spodoptera* spp.) and corn earworms (*Helicoverpa zea*), which taste like the corn they've been eating.

Other insect larvae make great meals too. Waxworms (*Galleria mellonella*) are a pest in beehives. Entomophagists say they are tasty when served roasted or fried. Silkworm pupae (*Bombyx mori*)—a by-product of the silk industry—are steamed, seasoned, and sold as a snack in China and Korea. And witchetty grubs, large white larvae of *Endoxyla leucomochla* and other moths, are a staple in Australia. They're skewered and roasted over hot coals until the skin crisps. Yum!

ENTOMARKET

When twelve-year-old Sam Broadbent of Maine asked his dad why his family didn't eat bugs, he didn't expect his question to launch a family business. But a couple of years later, Sam's father, Bill, and Sam's aunt Susan opened EntoMarket, an online marketplace devoted to edible insects.

Looking for curried crickets? EntoMarket has them, along with barbecued mealworms, giant water bugs, and chocolate-covered scorpions. Sam loves the *chapulines*. They are a mildly spicy alternative to potato chips, he says, and make great filling for tacos and burritos.

Sam's sister Julia says her favorite lunch snacks are crunchy roasted mealworms—barbecue or salt-and-vinegar flavors. She also likes cheese-flavored silkworm chrysalises that have the texture and taste of small snack crackers. At first, her friends at school thought eating bugs was weird. Julia would dare them to try just one. "After a while they decide they like them," she says.

Bill Broadbent likes cricket chips because they are a healthy snack. They taste like nacho chips, he says. The online market also offers ants, mopane and bamboo worms, cricket cookie mix, and other insect goodies.

MEALWORM TACOS

This taco recipe is a great way to introduce mealworms or other grubs into your diet.

1 tablespoon olive oil

¹/₂ onion, peeled and chopped

1 garlic clove, peeled and minced

¹/₂ cup mild or sweet peppers, seeded and diced

2 fresh tomatoes, diced

1 teaspoon oregano

1 teaspoon cumin

1 teaspoon coriander

1 teaspoon chili powder

1 can (16 ounces) of black beans, rinsed and drained

³/₄ cup fresh mealworms

¹/₄ cup water (approximately)

taco shells (or tortillas for soft tacos)

Toppings

chopped lettuce and other greens (spinach, lamb's-quarter, or garlic mustard)

grated cheese such as cheddar, Colby, or Monterey Jack (or one package of shredded taco cheese)

salsa or hot sauce

plain yogurt

guacamole

1. Heat olive oil in a large frying pan over medium heat. Sauté onion and garlic.

2. Stir in peppers, tomatoes, and spices and continue cooking a couple of minutes while the tomatoes soften.

3. Add beans and mealworms and a bit of water (up to ¹/₄ cup) to help the flavors blend. Let simmer about 5 minutes.

4. To assemble the tacos, fill each taco shell or tortilla with the meat mixture and add the toppings of your choice.

Many of EntoMarket's products are imported from around the world—China, Thailand, and Mexico. "People from all over the world have always eaten insects," Broadbent says. "Our southern neighbors in Mexico enjoy over 200 different bugs." He's hoping that as interest grows in the United States and Canada, he'll be able to sell insect foods from farms closer to home.

Nutritional and environmental advantages support entomophagy, Broadbent says. "We just have to overcome the emotional response." And it's not young people who say "yuck." When Broadbent offers roasted crickets, mealworms, or other insects to groups, nearly 80 percent of the kids will eat them. Only 40 percent of adults are brave enough to taste them.

CHAPTER 10
EATING ON THE WILD SIDE

CRICKETS AND MEALWORMS ARE TAME COMPARED TO THE MORE EXOTIC ARTHROPODS PEOPLE EAT: SPIDERS, SCORPIONS . . . even cockroaches. It's best to avoid eating urban roaches hanging out behind garbage cans. But according to Seattle-based bug chef David George Gordon, in general, cockroaches are delicious and nutritious. Some people say that when fried, Madagascar hissing cockroaches (*Gromphadorhina portentosa*) taste like crunchy fried chicken.

Termites (classified as the suborder Isoptera) are closely related to cockroaches. They too are often considered pests. And yet many of the more than two thousand termite species are edible, delicious, and nutritious. Termites are considered good food in more than two dozen countries in Africa, South America, and Asia. They are high in protein and a great source of vitamins A and C.

In rural areas, certain types of termites construct huge mounds using a mixture of dirt, saliva, and dung. The termites live in a nest at the base of the mound. To harvest the insects, people first dig a hole near a termite mound. Then they burn bundles of grass near the termite mound to bring out the termites, which are attracted to the light. As the termites come out of their nest, the termite hunters herd the insects into the hole and collect them there.

Termites build impressive mounds, building their nests at the base or underneath. Fried, steamed, and roasted termites are popular for eating in many parts of the world. Termites are also used in traditional medicines in some areas.

People fry, steam, or roast termites. Or they may boil them and then dry them in the sun or smoke them. Sometimes they pound or grind sun-dried termites into a powder and mix in other ingredients to make meat loaf, sausages, or muffins. Termites are high in nutritious fats too. People use termite oil (collected after frying the termites or by pressing dried termites) to fry other foods.

Humans may also benefit from termites in other ways. For example, certain types of termites are popular in traditional medicines in Brazil to treat ailments such as sore throats, coughs, and asthma. Many termite species live underground and have developed chemical resistance to disease-causing bacteria, viruses, and fungus in the soil. Recent medical experiments tested termite hemolymph—the insects' equivalent to blood—and found that it can kill certain bacteria. Compounds from some species of termites appear to be effective even against bacteria that are resistant to conventional antibiotic drugs.

BEETLE SOUP, *ZAZAMUSHI*, AND MORE

Nearly 150 years ago, beetles were becoming a huge problem in France. Cockchafers (*Melolontha* spp.) had invaded farmers' fields in the Normandy region of western France. The regional government wanted to exterminate the bugs. But a French senator had a better idea: eat the beetles. He published a recipe for cockchafer soup that was so scrumptious that it became a local delicacy.

Cockchafers are members of the Scarabaeidae (or scarab) family. All the beetles in this family—including June bugs (also called June beetles), Japanese beetles, chafers, and rhinoceros beetles—are edible and delectable.

Cockchafers (a type of beetle) are crispy and crunchy in salads and chip dip or on pizzas. Give them a try!

HOW TO CATCH JAPANESE BEETLES

Japanese beetles (*Popillia japonica*) are about one-half inch (1.5 cm) long with metallic-green bodies and coppery wing covers. They are active during the day and love roses, beans, grapes, and raspberries. They hang out in sunny places, gathering at the tops of plants where they chew on the leaves, flowers, and fruits.

The best time to collect Japanese beetles is in the morning when they move more slowly. When disturbed from a perch on a plant, the beetles let go and fall to the ground. Using this knowledge, you can make a beetle trap out of a soda bottle. Here's how:

What You Need
- scissors
- 1 plastic soda bottle, 2 liters, or about 2 quarts
- 1 Ping-Pong ball or paper towel

1. Using scissors, cut the bottle below the shoulder. The top piece will look sort of like a funnel.

2. Turn the top piece upside down, and put the narrow mouth of the funnel inside the other piece of the bottle. Then you have a collector.

3. Hold the collector in one hand beneath the leaves or flowers where beetles are feeding. Use your other hand to knock the beetles off the plant and into the collector.

4. When you've collected all the beetles you want, plug the opening of the bottle with a Ping-Pong ball or a wadded paper towel.

CRISP AND CRUNCHY BEETLE CROUTONS

Roasted Japanese beetles make great salad croutons. Add them to snack mixes, soups, and stews. Sprinkle them over salad or pizza. Crush them and stir into chip dip. Sprinkle over buttered popcorn. And just as with crickets, put the beetles into a ziplock plastic bag and chill them in the freezer for at least 20 minutes before cooking them.

1. While the beetles are chilling, whisk some Secret Bug Sauce (see page 87).

2. Fill a 2-quart (1.8 L) saucepan halfway with water and bring to a boil.

3. Place chilled beetles into a colander, and rinse them in cold water before pouring them into the boiling water. Gently boil them for 5 minutes.

4. Drain the cooked beetles, and soak them in Secret Bug Sauce overnight. For plain beetles, skip this step and let them air-dry before roasting.

5. To roast, preheat the oven to 225°F (110°C).

6. Spread the beetles on a lightly oiled cookie sheet, and bake for about 40 minutes. They are done when you can crush them with a spoon. If they're not crispy enough, continue roasting for another 10 minutes. Then they are ready to eat.

Beetles are also so plentiful that you can eat them without worrying about threatening their survival. They are tasty when marinated and then roasted or toasted. Toss them into salads as crouton substitutes, sprinkle them in brownie batter, or pop them into a snack mix to share with friends.

Looking for fast food? Check out dragonflies and damselflies, members of the biological Odonata family. They can fly at speeds of 35 miles (56 km) per hour. To catch them, dragonfly hunters on the Indonesian island of Bali spread sticky sap on the end of a thin, flexible stick. They tie this stick to a long, sturdy pole and then swish the pole through the air as though they are fishing. Unwary dragonflies and damselflies stick to the sap. The hunters remove their catch, clean off the sap, and then take off the insects' wings. Dragonflies and damselflies can be fried, roasted over hot coals, or cooked in coconut milk with garlic, ginger, onions, and chili peppers. Some people dip them in egg and seasoned breading or in tempura batter before frying.

People also eat the larvae of dragonflies as well as those of damselflies, caddisflies, stoneflies, and dobsonflies. Unlike their airborne parents, these larvae are aquatic. They live in the water for up to three years, spending most of their time under rocks and debris. The larvae devour other aquatic insects, tadpoles, and even tiny fish. In Japan people refer to these aquatic larvae as *zazamushi. Zaza* represents the sound of the flowing water in which they live, and *mushi* means "insects." *Zazamushi* hunters shuffle through the water, kicking over stones and picking up the larvae with chopsticks. For larger harvests, bug hunters set up nets in a stream and then walk upstream where they dislodge stones using large rakes. The larvae float downstream and are trapped by the nets. *Zazamushi* are gritty because they live in stream sediments. Before cooking, chefs rinse the insects to get all the grit out. Restaurants in Tokyo sell *zazamushi* simmered in a mix of soy sauce and sugar.

THE MORE LEGS THE MERRIER

There comes a time when an entomophagist wonders whether six legs are enough. Why not try a tarantula? After all, folks living in Cambodia and Venezuela enjoy eating these hairy eight-legged critters. Among the Piaroa people of Venezuela, children as young as five hunt tarantulas in the jungle and roast them over a fire. The spider they prefer is *Theraphosa blondi,* sometimes called the Goliath tarantula, or the South American Goliath birdeater. It can grow to the size of a large dinner plate, more than 1 foot (0.3 m) across.

In Cambodia, people call tarantulas *a-ping.* Farmers there collect a local species, *Haplopelma albostriatum,* or the Thai zebra tarantula, to sell at city markets. In Phnom Penh, the capital, restaurants serve fried tarantula.

Try a scorpion lollipop! Depending on where you live, you can find them at gas station convenience stores and even airport gift shops. Or you can buy them online.

And the town of Skuon is famous for street vendors who sell delicious fried tarantulas.

No matter where, hunting tarantulas has its dangers. The spider has large fangs that can deliver a painful bite. In addition, tarantula hairs can sting the skin and cause irritation. Before eating the spiders, cooks singe (briefly burn) the hairs off. The fangs can be used as toothpicks—handy! Tarantulas taste like their arthropod relatives, shrimp or crabs.

If your taste runs more toward lobster, consider the hairy desert scorpion. Bug Chef David George Gordon eats these critters from the American Southwest. He says the tail and claws are the best meat of a scorpion, as in a lobster—just be sure to avoid the venomous stinger. Half a world away from the southwestern desert, in China, scorpion on a stick is a popular snack. Cooks stir-fry and season small scorpions, which they sell in street markets. Westerners describe the taste of these scorpion snacks as similar to chicken skin from spicy fried chicken.

For most people in the United States, scorpions (like most other entomophagic fare) are a novelty. One way to eat them is in candy. You may see displays of colorful, fruit-flavored scorpion lollipops—each with a fully edible scorpion visible inside—at gift shops and gas stations across the United States. So keep a sharp eye out!

From cricket tacos and dandelion pancakes to kudzu salsa and roasted nutria, Americans are learning to be climate-savvy about the way they eat. Whether starting small with dandelion greens or going wild with *zazamushi,* anyone can take a bite out of climate change, global hunger, and agricultural pollution. You can make a difference.

GROW YOUR OWN GRUBS

It's tough to find live mealworms for human consumption. But you can grow your own with mealworms from a pet food store. Check pet and farm supply stores for wheat bran mealworm bedding. These beetle larvae (*Tenebrio molitor*) are common pantry pests and are easy to raise. Be sure to ask permission from an adult in your house before you get started with this project.

WHAT YOU NEED

- 1 marker pen
- 4 shoebox-sized plastic bins up to 16 x 11 x 6 inches (41 cm x 28 cm x 15 cm) with lids
- hammer and nail, or scissors
- stapler, hot glue gun, or duct tape
- pieces of window screen or mosquito netting
- 5 pounds (2.3 kg) of rolled oats, wheat bran, and/or cornmeal
- Cheerios or cornflakes (optional)
- slices of apple, carrots, potato, cucumber, and/or watermelon rinds
- 100 to 500 live mealworms
- 1 small mesh strainer or sieve

1. Before you get your mealworms, you need to make them a home. Use a marker pen to label each bin for each stage of the life cycle of the mealworm: eggs, larvae, pupae, and adult.

2. Using a hammer and nail, punch a bunch of holes in the lids. This lets in air for the mealworms to breathe. If you prefer, you can use a pair of scissors to cut out a section from the center of each lid and then staple, glue, or tape some screening over it.

3. Fill the bin labeled "larvae" with wheat bran or other grain to a depth of 1.5 to 2 inches (4 to 5 cm). If you're using oatmeal, grind it in a blender to make smaller pieces for the bedding. You may also mix wheat bran with ground oats and cornmeal, and add smashed cornflakes or Cheerios. Mealworms love grains.

4. Put slices of fruit, carrot, potato, cucumber, and/or watermelon rind around the surface to provide moisture for the mealworms. You'll be checking the containers daily and replacing the fruit and vegetables when they dry up, so make sure they aren't chopped too small to handle easily.

5. Before you add the mealworms to their new home, chill them in the refrigerator (not freezer) for an hour. This slows them down, without killing them, and makes it easier to inspect them. Spread them out on a cookie tray. Healthy mealworms look like thick-skinned yellowish caterpillars with six legs. Remove the dead ones (dark) and any larvae that are black with spiky hairs—they are not mealworms. Separate out the pupae (they look like wiggly whitish aliens) and the dark-colored adult beetles.

6. Place the mealworms (larvae) in the bin you prepared for them in step 3. Place any pupae you find in the empty bin labeled "pupae." If you have adult beetles, then put them in a bin set up the same way as the bin for larvae: with a bedding of wheat bran, cornmeal, ground oats, or grain mix and some sliced fruit and vegetables. Put the lids securely on the bins. Mealworms don't wander far if they escape, but the lids keep other insects from invading their home.

7. Put the bins in a warm place inside, away from drafty windows and doors, so the mealworms will grow quickly. Check your mealworm farm at least twice a week. (Some people check their mealworms every day.) Take out any dried, molding, or rotting fruit, stir the bedding, and add more ground grains and fresh slices of fruits and vegetables as needed. Mealworms spend eight to ten weeks as larvae and molt (shed their skin) ten to twenty times during that period. Don't worry about removing shed skins. The larvae will take care of them by eating them.

8. As you find pupae, put them in their bin so the mealworms don't eat them. After one to three weeks, the pupae will complete their metamorphosis and emerge as adult beetles. Remove adults so they don't eat the pupae, and put them in the "adult" bin.

9. Adult beetles are about one-half inch (13 mm) long. They can't fly, but they can run fast. Females lay about forty eggs per day for two to three months. The eggs are hard to see because they are tiny. It would take twenty lined up in a row to equal 1 inch (2.5 cm). They get buried in the grainy bedding too. Every two weeks, remove the grain bedding in the adult bugs' bin. By this time, the females will have laid eggs. Put that bedding (which will have the eggs in it) into the empty "eggs" bin. Be sure to add fresh bedding to the adult bugs' bin.

10. It takes about twelve days for eggs to hatch. For the first few weeks after hatching, the mealworm larvae will be too tiny to see. Check on them daily. During bin checks, take out those that are large enough to see and put them in the "larvae" bin. Use a spoon or sieve to move the larvae.

11. Stir the bedding in the mealworm bins from time to time. Clean them out every four weeks. To do this, use a sieve to remove the mealworms and put them in a large bowl or plastic tub for a few minutes. Empty and wash their bin with warm water. Dry well. Then add a new layer of grain bedding and slices of fruits and vegetables, and put the mealworms back. As for the used bedding, mealworm poop makes good fertilizer for gardens or can be added to compost.

12. Wait until the second generation of mealworms hatches before harvesting them for food. Then select the plumpest larvae for eating. Leave some in the bin to become adults so they can lay eggs. Your minilivestock farm will be off to a good start.

FINE DINING FOR ENTOMOPHAGISTS

Restaurants come and go, and many change their menus regularly, so it is always advisable to check before you go. But for enthusiastic entomophagists looking for bug-serving restaurants, here are some places to check out in your travels.

ASIA

Cambodia
- Phnom Penh
  Romdeng restaurant (tarantulas and more)
  http://tree-alliance.org/our-restaurants/romdeng.php?mm=or&sm=rd

- Siem Reap
  Bugs Cafe
  http://bugs-cafe.e-monsite.com/

Japan
- Tokyo
  The Mandarin Oriental Tokyo Bar (*zazamushi*)
  Review at http://damonbanks.com/gourmet-insects-mandarin-oriental
  -tokyo/

- Tokyo
  Nong Inlay
  http://nong-inlay.com/
  Review at www.timeout.com/tokyo/restaurants/nong-inlay

South Korea
- Seoul
  Papillon's Kitchen
  http://www.keilab.org/
  Review at http://koreabizwire.com/insect-restaurant-opens-in
  -seoul/52260

Thailand
- Bangkok
  Insects in the Backyard (wide variety)
  http://www.insectsinthebackyard.com/

EUROPE

United Kingdom
- London, England
  Archipelago Restaurant
  http://www.archipelago-restaurant.co.uk/

- Pembrokeshire, Wales
  Grub Kitchen
  http://www.grubkitchen.co.uk/

Netherlands
- The Buggie (a kitchen on wheels)
  https://www.bugalicious.nl/en/home/

NORTH AMERICA

Canada
- Toronto
  Cookie Martinez
  http://www.cookiemartinez.com

Mexico
- Mexico City
  La Cocina de San Juan
  https://www.facebook.com/La-Cocina-de-San-Juan
  -1470496716313275/
  Review at https://theculturetrip.com/north-america/mexico/articles
  /the-best-places-to-try-edible-insects-in-mexico-city/

- Mexico City
  Nicos
  https://www.nicosmexico.mx/
  Review at https://www.forbes.com/sites/cheryltiu/2016/10/11/ants
  -grasshoppers-and-worms-where-to-eat-insects-in-mexico-citys-fine
  -dining-restaurants/#3bb734ac4000

United States
- Chicago, IL
  Sticky Rice Northern Thai Cuisine
  http://stickyricethai.com/index10.php

- Los Angeles, CA
  Guelaguetza
  http://www.ilovemole.com/

- New Orleans, LA
  Bug Appétit snack bar (at the Audubon Butterfly Garden and
  Insectarium)
  https://audubonnatureinstitute.org/insectarium/explore
  -insectarium/insectarium-exhibits/401-bug-appetit

- New York, NY
  The Black Ant
  https://www.theblackantnyc.com/

- Seattle, WA
  Nue
  http://www.nueseattle.com/

- Washington, DC
  Oyamel
  http://www.oyamel.com

METRIC CONVERSIONS

Cooks in the United States measure both liquids and solids by volume, based on the 8-ounce cup and the tablespoon. The metric system also measures liquids by volume, but measures solids by their weight. To convert from US tablespoons and other volume measurements to metric liters and milliliters is straightforward using this chart.

With solids, because different substances have different weights—one cup of rice doesn't weigh the same as a cup of chopped celery, for example—many cooks who use the metric system have kitchen scales to weigh different ingredients, and recipes in those countries using the metric system provide the weights. This chart provides a starting point for basic conversions.

TEMPERATURE*

212°F	=	100°C (boiling point of water)
225°F	=	110°C
250°F	=	120°C
275°F	=	135°C
300°F	=	150°C
325°F	=	160°C
350°F	=	180°C
375°F	=	190°C
400°F	=	200°C

*To convert temperature in Fahrenheit to Centigrade, or Celsius, subtract 32 and multiply by 0.56.

LIQUID VOLUME

1 teaspoon (tsp.)	=	5.0 milliliters (mL)
1 tablespoon (tbsp.)	=	15.0 milliliters
1 fluid ounce (oz.)	=	30.0 milliliters
1 cup (c.)	=	240 milliliters
1 pint (pt.)	=	473 milliliters
1 quart (qt.)	=	0.9 liters (L)
1 gallon (gal.)	=	3.8 liters

MASS (WEIGHT)

1 ounce (oz.)	=	28 grams (g)
8 ounces	=	227 grams
1 pound (lb.), or 16 ounces	=	0.5 kilograms (kg)
2.2 pounds	=	1 kilogram

LENGTH

¼ inch (in.)	=	0.6 centimeters (cm)
½ inch	=	1.25 centimeters
1 inch	=	2.5 centimeters

SOURCE NOTES

12 Philip Stark, telephone interview with author (SH), March 16, 2017.

13 Ibid.

13 Ibid.

14 Patti Pitcher, telephone interview with author (SH), January 18, 2017.

14 Ibid.

47 Joe Roman, interview with author (CM), June 1, 2017.

56 Jordyn Chace, e-mail communication with author (CM), June 24, 2017.

56–57 Ibid.

57 Ibid.

61 Jackson Landers, "How to Stop an Invasion of the Easiest Fish in the World to Catch," *Wild Things: Slate's Animal Blog*, November 18, 2013, http://www.slate .com/blogs/wild_things/2013/11/18/asian_carp_in_great_lakes_call_them_silver _fin_and_eat_them.html.

62 "Why Not Eat Invasive Species?" Miya's Sushi, accessed November 21, 2017, http://www.miyassushi.com/mission/.

71 Philippe Parola, "Chef Philippe on Marketing Nutria," Chef Philippe Parola, accessed November 21, 2017, http://www.chefphilippe.com/nutria.html.

82 Esther Lee, "Shailene Woodley Eats Bugs, Thinks the 'Future of Food Is in Insects,'" *US Weekly*, March 26, 2015, https://www.usmagazine.com/celebrity -news/news/shailene-woodley-eats-bugs-future-of-food-insects-2015263/.

82 Celebrity, "Angelina Jolie Admits Her Kids Eat Crickets 'Like Doritos,'" Huffpost, last modified September 18, 2011, https://www.huffingtonpost.com/entry /angelina-jolie-kids-eat-bugs-video_n_902477.html.

83 Leviticus 11: 22 (New International Version), accessed March 28, 2018, https://www.biblegateway.com/passage/?search=Leviticus+11.

83 Mark 1:6; Matthew 3:4–6, accessed March 28, 2018, https://www.biblegateway .com/passage/?search=Mark+1%3A6%3B+Matthew+3%3A4%E2%80%936& version=NIV.

84   Sunan Ibn Majah, vol. 4, bk. 28, Hadith 3222 (English reference); bk 28, Hadith 3343 (Arabic reference), accessed March 28, 2018, https://sunnah.com/ibnmajah/28.

90   Jeanette Brown, telephone interview with author (SH), February 28, 2017.

91   "Technology," Aspire Food Group, accessed November 21, 2017, http://www.aspirefg.com/technology.aspx.

91   Jeanette Brown, telephone interview with author (SH), February 28, 2017.

95   Julia Broadbent, telephone interview with author (SH), January 31, 2017.

97   Bill Broadbent, e-mail communication with author (SH), June 22, 2017.

97   Bill Broadbent, telephone interview with author (SH), January 31, 2017.

GLOSSARY

arthropod: an animal within the phylum Arthropoda, which includes insects, arachnids, and crustaceans. These animals have external skeletons, segmented bodies, and six or more jointed legs.

biomass: the amount of living material in a specific area

bug: a general term to refer to various members of the phylum Arthropoda, including six-legged insects (ants, beetles, butterflies, crickets, and flies), eight-legged arachnids (including spiders and scorpions), millipedes, and centipedes

climate change: an alteration in prevailing weather conditions, in particular the change in Earth's climate starting in the mid to late twentieth century. Most scientists agree that this is caused by high volumes of carbon dioxide and other gases in the atmosphere resulting from human use of fossil fuels.

competition: in the science of ecology, the interactions among plants or animals in obtaining limited resources such as land, water, sunlight, and food

diversity: the variety or range of living organisms within a particular habitat or in the world. Scientists sometimes refer to the concept as biodiversity or biological diversity.

ecosystem: a natural community consisting of interacting living organisms and their physical habitat or environment

enteric fermentation: part of the digestive process of plant-eating ruminants (cows, goats, sheep, bison, and deer), which breaks down plant materials into usable nutrients and produces methane as a by-product

entomophagy: the practice of eating insects

exotic: in biology, this term refers to a plant or animal that originates in a distant or foreign place

extinct: no longer existing, as in a species with no living members

feral: wild, usually referring to escaped domestic animals that have reverted to a wild state

food desert: neighborhoods, often in low-income areas, that lack stores or markets that sell healthful foods such as fresh fruits and vegetables

forage: to search for food in nature, especially over a wide area

greenhouse gases: substances in Earth's atmosphere, including carbon dioxide and methane, that absorb radiation from the sun without allowing heat to escape. The effect warms the planet like a greenhouse made of glass, which traps sunlight for growing plants in cold weather.

grubs: larvae of insects, particularly beetles

habitat: the place where an organism normally lives; its natural environment

herbicide: a substance used to kill unwanted plants

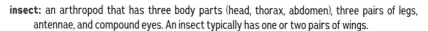

insect: an arthropod that has three body parts (head, thorax, abdomen), three pairs of legs, antennae, and compound eyes. An insect typically has one or two pairs of wings.

introduced species: an organism that has been brought into a new location or ecosystem with human help, either intentionally or accidentally

invasive species: an introduced organism that spreads beyond its initial area of introduction and often causes economic or environmental harm or harm to human health

invasivore: someone who eats invasive species

larva: the immature stage of an insect that goes through complete metamorphosis

locavore: someone who eats food grown or produced close to home, generally within 100 miles (161 km)

metamorphosis: a complete change of form as an insect moves from one life stage to another. For example, a butterfly starts out as an egg, which hatches into a larva (caterpillar), then changes into a pupa (chrysalis), from which the adult butterfly emerges.

mycorrhizal fungi: beneficial fungi growing in association with roots of plants. The fungi act as extensions to the plant root systems, increasing their absorptive area.

omnivore: an animal that eats both plants and animals

outcompete: in the science of ecology, when one species is more successful than another in using available, limited resources such as land area and food

pest: an organism that damages property, interferes with economic activities such as agriculture and forestry, or is harmful to the health of humans or domestic animals

pesticide: a substance used to repel or kill pests. The term applies to insecticides, herbicides, fungicides, and other substances.

pupa: an inactive intermediate stage in the metamorphosis of an insect, between larva and adult, during which the insect undergoes radical changes in structure

rhizome: a horizontal underground stem of a plant that produces roots and sends up shoots

ruminant: a cud-chewing mammal that gets its nutrition by fermenting the plants it has eaten in a specialized second stomach before further digestion

succulent: a plant with thick, fleshy leaves that store water

symbiotic: mutually beneficial interaction between two different organisms living together

vegetarian: a person who does not eat meat. Some vegetarians also exclude other animal products from their diet, such as eggs or dairy.

weed: a plant that people consider undesirable, or unwanted, in certain situations or places

SELECTED BIBLIOGRAPHY

"ASPIRE Cricket Farm," video, 1:58. Aspire Food Group. Accessed November 21, 2017. https://cdnapisec.kaltura.com/index.php/extwidget/preview/partner_id/2285551/uiconf_id/39642171/entry_id/O_qtlgedal/embed/dynamic.

Borel, Brooke. "The Rise of the Incredible Edible Insect." *Popular Science*, May 12, 2015. http://www.popsci.com/rise-incredible-edible-insect.

Can't Beat 'Em, Eat 'Em. Accessed November 18, 2017. http://www.cantbeatemeatem.us/.

"The Day and The Life of Mr. Dom, a Cricket Farmer." *Matt Prindle* (blog). Accessed November 21, 2017. http://mattprindle.com/day-life-cricket-farmer/.

Deane, Green. Eat the Weeds. Accessed November 21, 2017. http://www.eattheweeds.com/.

Fears, Darryl. "The Dirty Dozen: 12 of the Most Destructive Invasive Animals in the United States." *Washington Post*, February 23, 2015. https://www.washingtonpost.com/news/energy-environment/wp/2015/02/23/like-most-invasive-species-pythons-are-in-the-u-s-to-stay/?utm_term=.56b50c4136c5.

Garfield, Leanna. "4 Ways Your Dinner Will Look Different in 2025." *Business Insider*, December 4, 2015. http://www.techinsider.io/alternatives-to-meat-in-2025-2015-11.

Goodyear, Dana. *Anything That Moves: Renegade Chefs, Fearless Eaters, and the Making of a New American Food Culture*. New York: Riverhead Books, 2013.

"Greenhouse Gas (GHG) Emissions." US Environmental Protection Agency. Accessed November 21, 2017. https://www.epa.gov/ghgemissions.

Hoddle, Mark S. Center for Invasive Species Research, University of California, Riverside. Accessed November 21, 2017. http://cisr.ucr.edu/invasive_species_faqs.html.

"How Much Water Does It Take to Grow a Hamburger?" US Geological Survey. Accessed June 26, 2017. https://water.usgs.gov/edu/activity-watercontent.html.

Mark, Jason. "Weeds—They're What's for Dinner." *Earth Island Journal*, April 8, 2015. http://www.earthisland.org/journal/index.php/elist/eListRead/weeds_theyre_whats_for_dinner/.

Matsumoto, Nancy. "Have You Ever Tried to Eat a Feral Pig?" *Atlantic*, July 11, 2013. https://www.theatlantic.com/national/archive/2013/07/have-you-ever-tried-to-eat-a-feral-pig/277666/.

McEowen, Anne. "Louses & Locusts." *Rural Missouri*, July 2009, http://www.ruralmissouri.org/09pages/09JulyRiley.html.

Menzel, Peter, and Faith D'Aluisio. *Man Eating Bugs: The Art and Science of Eating Insects*. Berkeley, CA: Ten Speed, 1998.

Morthland, John. "A Plague of Pigs in Texas." *Smithsonian*, January 2011. http://www.smithsonianmag.com/science-nature/a-plague-of-pigs-in-texas-73769069/.

Parry, Wynne. "On the Menu: Taking a Bite Out of Invasive Species." *LiveScience*, March 25, 2011. https://www.livescience.com/13426-invasive-species-invasivory-recipes-diet.html.

Peters, Adele. "This Giant Automated Cricket Farm Is Designed to Make Bugs a Mainstream Source of Protein." *Fast Company,* August 21, 2017. https://www.fastcompany.com /40454212/this-automated-cricket-farm-is-designed-to-make-bugs-a-mainstream -source-of-protein.

Pieters, A. J. "Kudzu: A Forage Crop for the Southeast." USDA Leaflet 91 (1932). Accessed June 12, 2017. https://archive.org/stream/kudzuforagecropf91piet/kudzuforagecropf91piet.

Shemkus, Sarah. "Eat an Invasive Species for Dinner." *Atlantic,* April 8, 2016. https://www .theatlantic.com/science/archive/2016/04/invasive-lionfish/477570/.

Shute, Nancy. "Foraging the Weeds for Wild, Healthy Greens." *NPR,* April 18, 2011. http://www.npr .org/2011/04/18/135412640/foraging-the-weeds-for-wild-healthy-greens.

Swearingen, J., B. Slattery, K. Reshetiloff, and S. Zwicker. *Plant Invaders of Mid-Atlantic Natural Areas.* 4th ed. Washington, DC: National Park Service and U.S. Fish and Wildlife Service, 2010. https://www.lhprism.org/document/plant-invaders-mid-atlantic-natural-areas.

van Huis, Arnold, Henk van Gurp, Marcel Dicke, Francoise Takken-Kaminker, and Diane Blumenfeld-Schaap. *The Insect Cookbook: Food for a Sustainable Planet.* New York: Columbia University Press, 2014.

van Huis, Arnold, Joost Van Itterbeek, Harmke Klunder, Esther Mertens, Afton Halloran, Giulia Muir, and Paul Vantomme. *Edible Insects: Future Prospects for Food and Feed Security.* FAO Forestry Paper 171. Rome: Food and Agriculture Organization of the United Nations, 2013. http://www.fao.org/docrep/018/i3253e/i3253e.pdf.

Vasquez, Kristen Rasmussen de. "Foraged Food Trend Is Part Epicurean, Part Environmental." *Food & Nutrition,* July/August 2016. http://www.foodandnutrition.org/July-August-2016 /Wild-Eats/.

Whitty, Julia. "Listen to the Lionfish: What Invasive Species Are Trying to Tell Us." *Mother Jones,* January/February 2009. http://www.motherjones.com/environment/2009/02/what -invasive-species-are-trying-tell-us/.

FURTHER INFORMATION

BOOKS

Cranshaw, Whitney. *Garden Insects of North America.* 2nd ed. Princeton, NJ: Princeton University Press, 2018.

Elias, Thomas, and Peter Dykeman. *Edible Wild Plants: A North American Field Guide to Over 200 Natural Foods.* 10th ed. New York: Sterling, 2009.

Gordon, David George. *The Eat-a-Bug Cookbook: 40 Ways to Cook Crickets, Grasshoppers, Ants, Water Bugs, Spiders, Centipedes, and Their Kin.* Berkeley, CA: Ten Speed, 2013.

Grassi, M. K. *Let's Eat Bugs! A Thought-Provoking Introduction to Edible Insects for Adventurous Teens and Adults.* Charleston, SC: CreateSpace Independent Publishing Platform, 2014.

Kallas, John. *Edible Wild Plants: Wild Foods from Dirt to Plate.* Layton, UT: Gibbs Smith, 2010.

Landers, Jackson. *Eating Aliens: One Man's Adventures Hunting Invasive Animal Species.* North Adams, MA: Storey, 2012.

Martin, Daniella. *Edible: An Adventure into the World of Eating Insects and the Last Great Hope to Save the Planet.* New York: Houghton Mifflin Harcourt, 2014.

Monger, Karen. *Adventures in Edible Plant Foraging: Finding, Identifying, Harvesting, and Preparing Native and Invasive Wild Plants.* New York: Skyhorse, 2015.

Peterson, Lee Allen. *A Field Guide to Wild Edible Plants: Eastern and Central North America.* Boston: Houghton Mifflin Harcourt, 1999.

Ramos-Elorduy, Julieta. *Creepy Crawly Cuisine: The Gourmet Guide to Edible Insects.* Rochester, VT: Park Street, 1998.

Zachos, Ellen. *Backyard Foraging: 65 Familiar Plants You Didn't Know You Could Eat.* North Adams, MA: Storey, 2013.

Zimmern, Andrew. *Andrew Zimmern's Field Guide to Exceptionally Weird, Wild, & Wonderful Foods: An Intrepid Eater's Digest.* New York: Feiwel & Friends, 2012.

WEBSITES

Appalachian Forest Heritage Area (AFHA)

http://www.afha.us

The AFHA works to conserve, develop, and celebrate the history, culture, natural history, and forestry throughout West Virginia and Maryland. It hosts a garlic mustard challenge and provides a collection of recipes, "Garlic Mustard, from Pest to Pesto," available online at http://www.appalachianforest.us/garlic_mustard/gm_recipes.pdf.

Berkeley Open Source Food

http://forage.berkeley.edu/

This organization works on issues of food equity, sustainability, resilience, nutrition, biodiversity, and increasing the supply of fresh, affordable, nutritious, drought-resistant, low-carbon-impact greens. They also test urban soils in their area for toxicity.

Bugs for Dinner

http://www.bugsfordinner.com/

The mission of this organization is to change minds about eating insects. Visitors will find articles, videos, a blog, and a link to the online store EntoMarket.

Bugs You Can Eat

http://www.pbs.org/wgbh/nova/ants/bugs-nf.html

This is a helpful compilation of photographs and commentary by Peter Menzel and Faith D'Aluisio (authors of *Man Eating Bugs*), describing edible insects. An interactive version, also by Menzel and D'Aluisio, is available at http://www.pbs.org/wgbh/nova/nature/bugs-you -can-eat.html.

Can't Beat 'Em, Eat 'Em

http://www.cantbeatemeatem.us/

This website provides information about invasive species and recipes and guidance for eating them. It describes Chef Philippe Parola's campaign to bring invasive species to restaurants.

Center for a Livable Future

https://www.jhsph.edu/research/centers-and-institutes/johns-hopkins-center-for-a-livable -future/

This academic center at the Johns Hopkins School of Public Health is devoted to research, education, and community action, and its website compiles data and research results. Its work is driven by the principle that public health, diet, food production, and the environment are deeply interrelated, and that understanding these relationships is crucial to the future.

Eat Low Carbon Calculator
> http://eatlowcarbon.org/
> This website provides interactive quizzes and a carbon calculator to test your knowledge and determine carbon scores for various food choices.

Eat the Invaders
> http://eattheinvaders.org/
> Run by editor 'n' chef Joe Roman and encouraging people to "Fight Invasive Species, One Bite at a Time," this website offers information about edible invasive species, with recipes.

Eat the Weeds
> http://www.eattheweeds.com
> This foraging website provides basic information about edible weeds, plant profiles, photos, and more.

Food Climate Research Network
> http://www.fcrn.org.uk/
> The network based at the University of Oxford, England, collects and makes available scientific research and other information about the interrelated issues of food and climate change.

Global Garlic Mustard Field Survey
> http://www.garlicmustard.org/
> Help scientists learn more about invasive garlic mustard by becoming a citizen scientist. Participants in the garlic mustard survey help to count, measure, and report on locations and the extent of garlic mustard plants.

Institute for Applied Ecology
> https://appliedeco.org/invasive-species/
> This website provides information about an Oregon conservation organization working to restore natural ecosystems. It has developed a program called Eradication by Mastication and hosts an annual invasive species cook-off.

Louisiana Department of Wildlife & Fisheries Nutria for Human Consumption
> http://www.nutria.com/site14.php
> This section of a website developed by the State of Louisiana provides nutritional information, recipes, and helpful photographs for people interested in cooking and eating nutria.

Real Food Challenge
> http://realfoodchallenge.org/
> This website offers information about a program run by a national network of students to promote local, fair, and sustainable food systems, particularly on college and university campuses.

Reef Environmental Education Foundation (REEF)
> http://www.reef.org/about
> http://www.reef.org/lionfish/events
> REEF is an organization focused on conserving reef ecosystems and helping divers participate in monitoring and reporting on reef health. The website offers extensive information about collecting lionfish and events including collection dives and lionfish derbies.

VIDEOS AND DOCUMENTARIES

"Changing How We Eat: Crickets as Protein"
> TedX Manhattan. March 1, 2014.
> http://new.livestream.com/tedx/manhattan2014/videos/43853036
> In this talk at TedX Manhattan, Megan Miller discusses her work to promote use of cricket flour.

"Children Hunt World's Largest Venomous Spider for Dinner"
> BBC One, *Human Planet: Jungles.* January 27, 2011.
> https://www.youtube.com/watch?v=ra4WmE-joMQ
> Short documentary footage follows young members of the Piaroa people as they hunt, catch, and cook tarantulas in the jungle of Venezuela.

"Defeating Invaders by Eating Invaders."
> University of Vermont, University Communications. April 9, 2017.
> http://www.uvm.edu/~uvmpr/?Page=news&storyID=24373&category=ucommall
> The linked video reports on an invasive species dinner with University of Vermont students, including interviews with participants.

"Everything You Need to Know about Eating Insects"
> Telus/Storyhive. September 12, 2014.
> https://www.youtube.com/watch?v=95UGrXKDYL0
> This documentary about entomophagy features Meeru Dahwali, chef/owner of insect-serving restaurants in Vancouver, BC; Aspire Food Group cofounders Shobhita Soor and Jesse Pearlstein; and Dr. David Lau, Faculty of Medicine, University of Calgary.

"How to Make a Kudzu Vine Basket"
River Valley Survival and Bushcraft. September 30, 2015.
Part 1 https://youtu.be/Gdv3sZGENEI
Part 2 https://youtu.be/czD6r2rjpX0
In each seven-minute video, artists from River Valley Survival and Bushcraft weave kudzu vines into baskets.

"How to Make Paper from Plant Fibers"
Howcast.com. July 21, 2010.
https://youtu.be/jzps7M5neVw
This short video demonstrates how to make paper from the leaves of plants.

"Hunting and Eating Invasive Iguanas"
National Geographic, September 2, 2015.
https://www.youtube.com/watch?v=h0886du3XmM
This short video documentary focuses on invasive iguanas in Puerto Rico and efforts to control them, including by hunting and eating them.

"Mindfully Eating a Scorpion in China"
Eating Mindfully. May 12, 2014.
https://www.youtube.com/watch?v=x3DeBRmYlig&feature=youtu.be
This video documents tourists in China faced with scorpions on a stick. This experience is described further in a related article by Susan Albers, "How to Mindfully Eat a Scorpion." *Huffington Post*, July 15, 2014. http://www.huffingtonpost.com/dr-susan-albers/how -mindfully-eat-a-scorp_b_5321948.html.

"Silent Invaders, Episode 3: Asian Carp"
Wildlife Forever, with North American Fishing Club. February 16, 2011.
https://www.youtube.com/watch?v=6rF-STc3-Js
See silver carp jumping out of the water and into boats, and view descriptions of efforts to control this invasive species.

INDEX

PHOTO ACKNOWLEDGMENTS

Image credits: TheModernCanvas/Shutterstock.com, p. 1; Charoenkrung.Studio99/Shutterstock.com, p. 4; Danny E Hooks/Shutterstock.com, p. 6; North Wind Picture Archives/Alamy Stock Photo, p. 7; travelview/Shutterstock.com, p. 9; Independent Picture Service, pp. 11, 104; Imageman/Shutterstock.com, p. 12 (left); simona pavan/Shutterstock.com, p. 12 (right); © Ingrid Lawrence, p. 14; Jakob Valling/Getty Images, p. 16; John McDonnell/The Washington Post/Getty Images, p. 21; Laura Westlund/Independent Picture Service, pp. 22, 39, 52, 74 (all); mimohe/Shutterstock.com, p. 25; Marina Onokhina/Shutterstock.com, p. 29; MSnider/Shutterstock.com, p. 31; GlOck/Shutterstock.com, p. 33; fewerton/Shutterstock.com, p. 38; Eduard Kyslynskyy/Shutterstock.com, p. 41; Chuck Wagner/Shutterstock.com, p. 43; Dmytro Furman/Shutterstock.com, p. 45; Wikimedia Commons (public domain), p. 47; John Warburton-Lee Photography/Alamy Stock Photo, p. 48; WaterFrame/Alamy Stock Photo, p. 49; Jim West/Alamy Stock Photo, p. 50; Laura Dinraths/Shutterstock.com, p. 51; Joshua Brown on behalf of University of Vermont, p. 55; Jason Lindsey/Alamy Stock Photo, p. 60; Gary Porter/Milwaukee Journal Sentinel/TNS/Getty Images, p. 61; Mikeybpt/Wikimedia Commons (Share Alike 4.0), p. 62; AP Photo/Nam Y. Huh, p. 63; Tosh Brown/Alamy Stock Photo, p. 65; Swapan Photography/Shutterstock.com, p. 68; Csakanyl/Shutterstock.com, p. 69; Bruce MacQueen/Shutterstock.com, p. 70; pawopa3336/iStock/Getty Images, p. 73; andy kramer/Alamy Stock Photo, p. 75; Gewitterkind/iStock/Getty Images, p. 79; loonger/iStock/Getty Images, p. 83; © Miquel Gonzalez/laif/Redux, p. 85; Kathryn Scott/The Denver Post/Getty Images, pp. 89, 91; Universal Images Group North America LLC/Alamy Stock Photo, p. 93; The_Fairhead/Shutterstock.com, p. 94; Posnov/agency/Getty Images, p. 99; ullstein bild/Getty Images, p. 100.

Cover: Vasmila/Shutterstock.com; TheModernCanvas/Shutterstock.com.

ABOUT THE AUTHORS

Christy Mihaly writes nonfiction for young readers. She has published many books for the educational market, including titles about nature, technology, and math, as well as magazine articles, stories, poetry, and activities. Mihaly studied environmental policy at Dartmouth College and law at the University of California, Berkeley. She spent more than two decades working as an environmental lawyer in California before moving with her family to rural Vermont, where she currently enjoys writing under the supervision of her dog and cat. You can visit her website at www.christymihaly.com.

Sue Heavenrich writes about science and environmental issues and is passionate about insects. She has followed ants in the Arizona desert, tagged bumblebees in the Rocky Mountains, and tallied insects on Cocos Island, Costa Rica. When not writing, she collects data for researchers as a citizen scientist. Heavenrich lives in upstate New York with her family and an organic garden full of edible weeds and bugs.

Mihaly and Heavenrich met at a 2013 nonfiction writing workshop in Pennsylvania, hit it off, and began working together as writing colleagues over the Internet. The next time they crossed paths in person was at a 2015 writers' conference in Georgia, where they hatched the plan for this book over a snack of roasted crickets. And the rest is history.